Dedicated to Craig Brown who sadly passed away
during the writing of this book.

Craig was a kind and generous man whose contribution
will not be forgotten.

Published by Transform Sales International
Graham Hawkins
150 North Oatlands Rd
Yarrambat Victoria 3091
Australia

www.transformsales.com.au

Design: Charlotte Gelin Design
Illustrations: Charlotte Gelin Design
Printed in Australia by loveofbooks.com.au

National Library of Australia Cataloguing-in-Publication entry
Creator: Hawkins, Graham, author.
Title: Sales Transformation / Graham Hawkins.
ISBN: 9780646944012 (paperback)
Subjects: Sales management.
Sales promotion.
Success in business.
Dewey Number: 658.81

Contents

Foreword

As a kid, I had my heart set on becoming a professional sportsman, however that dream failed to materialize and I somehow found myself working in sales. For almost 3 decades I have worked in a variety of sales and sales leadership roles across a number of industries and during this time I have gained many insights into the art of selling. The majority of my career has been spent selling *big-ticket, long-sales-cycle* technology products and services business to business (B2B) in Australia, the UK and throughout South East Asia.

I vividly recall my very first role within a large IT company. It was 1996 and, after many years of trying to break down the doors, I had finally made it to the biggest game in town – *"enterprise software"*. This exciting new role came to me at a time when most software vendors were experiencing extraordinary growth, making massive profits and attracting all of the best sales talent available. Naturally, I was delighted to have finally landed a highly sought after sales role within the Australian branch of a global software vendor. To put this in some context, it was throughout the 1990s that almost every IT market globally was immersed in various stages of burgeoning, and sometimes irrational, growth. IT vendors (particularly software vendors) were spending billions of dollars on R&D in the hope of creating the next big disruptive innovation, whilst customers (IT end users) were constantly searching for the next technology breakthrough that could transform their businesses and provide them with a competitive advantage. The software industry was booming and there were large sales opportunities everywhere you looked.

During this unprecedented technology explosion, vendor sales people were afforded what I recall as being almost rock star status. Not only were these sales people earning massive commissions due to exploding sales growth but they were highly sought after for their 'bleeding edge' knowledge and access to game-changing R&D that vendors were investing in so heavily. Even here in Australia, as a software salesperson I was able pick up the phone and call almost any business – small, medium or large – and be instantly granted an appointment. The red carpet was metaphorically being rolled out to software vendor sales people, and this had never happened in my previous sales roles. This was largely due to the fact that it was still in the early days of the IT industry growth cycle at a point when customers desperately needed vendors to educate them on how technology could help them to reduce costs and enable their business growth. At this particular point in time, the vendors held all the cards.

Fast forward almost eighteen years to 2015 and everything has changed. Vendor sales personnel are no longer rock stars, and the balance of power has now shifted back in favor of the IT buyers (customers). In fact, the sad truth is that in many cases vendor sales people are now almost *'persona non grata'* with many customers. So, what has caused this enormous change?

It was around 2006 when I first began hearing senior IT executives (from within my customer accounts) stating that they **"need to do more business with less vendors"**. Intuitively I understood what this meant, but it wasn't until 2011, when working as the Director of Sales (Australia) for a large US based software organisation, that I was faced with a very concerning situation with one of our key Australian customers. The customer was Qantas Airways Limited and, like almost every airline globally, Qantas was desperately searching for any means by which they could drive down the cost structure of their business. One area of particular focus for Qantas was the increasingly cost-laden area of 'vendor management'. Put simply, as businesses have become more and more reliant on IT to run their operations, dealing with vast numbers of IT suppliers/vendors has become extremely complex, time consuming and therefore costly.

Despite what had been a long and mutually rewarding business relationship that had spanned over 15 years, I was informed by Qantas that my company (the vendor) was being *"downgraded on the 'vendor stack' and now categorized as a Tier 3 vendor"*. Whilst I didn't know exactly what that meant, I sensed that it was not good news. My contact at Qantas (Ms Prue Jacobson – then Head of Technology Procurement and Supplier Management) went on to explain that *"Qantas was in the process eliminating any Tier 3 vendors that were deemed as low priority, and seeking to identify a substitute product from another existing supplier (Tier 1 or 2)"*. This was definitely not good news.

Prue then explained to me that the alternative to being *"culled from the vendor stack"* was that my company was *"only going to be permitted to engage with Qantas through a Tier 1 or 'prime vendor'"*. In other words, my sales team would no longer be selling directly to our end-user, but instead via a third party partner organisation who would naturally expect to retain a margin from each and every sale that we made.

Both of these potential outcomes would mean a significant change in my sales execution plan and this represented a serious risk to our Australian-based business. It was on the back of this particular experience with Qantas that I began asking our other Australian-based customers about where my company was ranked on their 'vendor stack' and the feedback that I received was alarming to say the least. Almost every one of our existing customers was now moving in the same direction as Qantas, and this meant that my sales team and I were now headed into some unchartered waters.

Not surprisingly, many IT vendor organisations seem unaware of the rapidly changing nature of buyer behaviour within the markets that they supply. Well-established IT vendors have been enjoying the spoils of an extraordinarily long period of year-on-year growth and this past success has created a very inwardly focused view for many vendors. As high-tech markets continue to mature, barriers to entry come down, competition intensifies and many vendors are so focused on how they line up against their various competitors (in many cases, across multiple lines of business) that these same vendors are now unwittingly failing the first major test of business – understanding their market and customer requirements.

This book presents a number of important trends that are now impacting vendor sales organisations and it chronicles these industry shifts and the impact that they are now having on vendor sales departments. The upcoming pages will provide management executives with the rationale for an immediate review of their sales models and a complete rethink of their overall go-to-market planning.

To address some of these important changes, I have drawn on my own 27 years of experience to present my Top 10 Initiatives for *Sales Transformation*. Some of these initiatives will be easily understood and implemented and should provide some very quick wins for vendor sales leaders. However, some of the initiatives contained herein will require a more traditional approach to change management and there will no doubt be some resistance. Regardless, change is no longer coming – it's here!

This book aims to:

1. Highlight important changes in buyer behaviour, evolving customer requirements and the factors that are now driving vendors to change.

2. Outline a range of initiatives that vendors must now consider in order to transform their sales models.

3. Present empirical support for *Sales Transformation* directly from Australian-based enterprise customers.

4. Provide justification to vendors for the investment in *Sales Transformation*.

Introduction

IT vendors have had it *too good for too long* and the balance of power is shifting rapidly as we witness the rise of the customer-led economy. Adapting to this new customer-led environment is going to be a major challenge for vendors, many of whom must now rapidly transform their sales models to accommodate these important changes in buyer behaviour. The traditional buying cycle (now referred to as the *'buying journey'*) is now changing so dramatically with the maturing of the various IT markets that the traditional vendor salesperson can no longer influence customer decision-making the way that they once did. Put simply, the traditional role of the B2B salesperson is no longer relevant and yet many vendors seem oblivious to these important developments.

Global technology industries have grown so dramatically that we now have an oversupply of IT vendors which continues to create pressure on businesses to identify any means by which they can do *"more business with less vendors.* In most western developed economies such as Australia, many enterprise level businesses (large corporations) are now mandating to 'block' engagement with any 'new' or 'off-panel' vendors – insisting on finding a 'substitute' product from an existing (pre-approved) vendor, and this is now beginning to have a significant impact on the way in which IT buyers engage with their vendors.

It is my contention that one of the most misunderstood aspects of high tech sales within the current context is the extent to which each customer (IT buyer) categorizes it vendors into some sort of *'vendor stack'*. The following pages will discuss this concept in more detail, but to summarize, any vendor that is currently categorized by a customer as Tier 3, 4 or 5 is now facing some significant threats to their existing business models:

Specifically:

1. IT buyers are now seeking to rationalize vendors and cull any Tier 3 (or higher) vendors that may be deemed as 'non-essential'.

buyers will soon insist that Tier 3 (or higher) vendors must only engage via a 'Tier 1' or 'prime' vendor.

The seriousness of these abovementioned trends for vendor's sales operations cannot be overstated, particularly for smaller vendors who rarely ever reach the higher echelons of the *vendor stack*. Indeed, this is a very difficult time for start-up or single product vendors.

Added to these important changes in buyer behaviour is the on-going globalization of markets and the emerging technology megatrends, which are the principal enablers of this new customer-centric paradigm. These changes continue to impact on the way that organizations identify, procure and consume IT products and services. *Cloud Computing, Mobility, Virtualization, Managed Service Provision* (MSP) are all increasingly seen as effective enablers of change allowing customers to significantly lower the total cost of ownership for the IT products and services that they require to run their businesses. *Consumption-based* models that facilitate more flexible usage and payment options continue to gain traction with cost focused IT customers, and yet many IT vendors remained wedded to the legacy models of the past. Why? The simple answer to this question is that virtually no investment has gone into better understanding evolving customer needs, and when combined with the continued emphasis on short-term financial results this creates a dangerously blinkered approach by vendors that is no longer congruent with customer requirements.

It is now undeniable that existing vendor sales models are not keeping pace with these important shifts in buyer behaviour as IT buyers struggle with factors that contribute to higher costs. The traditional 'one-size-fits-all' B2B sales model is now dying and not before time. Vendor sales leaders must now acknowledge and adapt to these external change drivers and they must do it rapidly in order to survive into the future.

In the same way that the vast majority of record labels were caught napping when digital music first appeared as something that consumers might actually want, IT vendors that fail to rapidly transform their sales models will be saddled with larger, more cumbersome sales organizations that will continue to erode margins. Worse still, vendors that fail to quickly adapt to these changes will face the prospect of a shrinking customer base, along with rapid declines in top-line revenue and market share.

The writing of this book has provided me with the impetus to challenge much of what I have learned over the past 27 years, and I have attempted to critically analyze all the important issues outlined above from the point of view of an IT vendor. All the research that I have highlighted within these pages is congruent with my own personal experience in recent times. However, I felt that it was important to further test and validate some of these latest trends in the context of the local Australian market by speaking directly with some key enterprise IT buyers. During the research phase of this book, long form interviews were conducted with senior executives (mostly Procurement and Vendor Management) from inside six ASX listed corporations. Multiple interviews were also conducted with Australian-based senior executives from within a range of well-known IT vendor organisations.

The conclusions contained herein are very clear: *If buyers change how they buy, then sellers need to also change how they sell.* Vendor sales leaders must now recognize how all of this change within this globalized business context will undoubtedly impact their businesses. IT vendors that have not already begun, must urgently commence the process of rapid **Sales Transformation**.

Part One

MARKET EVOLUTION

The balance of power has undoubtedly shifted to increasingly powerful customers, and Part 1 of this book provides a very broad summary of some of the key trends that are now impacting IT businesses with a particular focus on the implications for vendor sales teams.

CHAPTER 1

Current Trends

Market Maturity

Broadly speaking, the global market for IT products and services, and the various sub-markets (segments), are now reaching a new level of maturity meaning that the industry is now well past the introductory and growth stages that are typical of the industry development lifecycle. With this new level of industry maturity comes increasingly educated customers who now have an unprecedented amount of data and information available at their fingertips.

Typical Industry Lifecycle

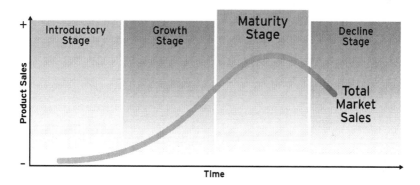

The hedonistic days of the 80s, and 90s, where technology growth was exploding in all directions, are now making way for a much more sedate and mature phase and, whilst new technology innovations continue to drive the disruptive change that fuels business growth, we are now definitely witnessing a new era of *'business as usual'* minus the irrational exuberance. Quite often mature businesses become restricted by their own complacency and arrogance which nearly always results in an insular focus which restricts growth. Some analysts are now saying that overall economic growth (world GDP) is exceeding the growth of many tech companies and whilst this sounds completely implausible to IT industry veterans like myself, declining growth is a perfectly natural by-product of market maturity. Commoditization is now a growing issue in most segments of IT, and this creates downward pressure on margins and profit whilst at the same time making the role of the sales person more difficult.

Putting the industry lifecycle aside for a moment, from a technology perspective we have reached a new era that some industry experts are calling the '3rd Platform'. Simply put, the 3rd Platform is the next phase of the IT revolution. The first platform that created explosive growth was centered on the *mainframe computer*. The second was the *personal computer* and the *client/server* architectures which dominated the IT landscape from 1985 to 2005. The so-called *3rd Platform* is being built upon mobile computing, social networking, cloud services, *Big Data* analytics, and something that industry pundits are now calling the *Internet-of-things* ('IoT').

As has always been the case, innovation continues to disrupt almost every area of the IT market, rendering some technologies (and vendors) redundant almost overnight, and this constant evolution of the industry and the shortening of product lifecycles means that the standard industry lifecycle curve (or *bell curve*) continues to push ever further to the right. Each successful innovation spawns a new level of creative destruction that generates a brand new bell curve (industry lifecycle) at the point where the old technology was made redundant. When this happens, a new wave of growth arises and participating vendor sales people, who are fortunate enough to find themselves in these emerging growth markets, often make a killing.

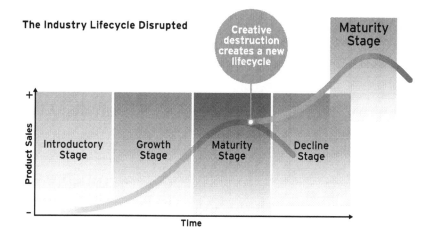

The Industry Lifecycle Disrupted

Creative destruction creates a new lifecycle

Maturity Stage

Product Sales

+

Introductory Stage

Growth Stage

Maturity Stage

Decline Stage

−

Time

More so than in any other industry, the pressure of disruptive innovation means that technology vendors are constantly searching for their next competitive differentiator. Almost every area of IT is now characterized by a certain degree of saturation and commoditization as the barriers-to-entry come down and more and more vendors flood into each market segment. It is this maturing of the IT industry that has led to the current over-supply of IT vendors and, depending on which definition you decide to use, there is no doubt that IT (in general) is now a consolidating market with some rapidly changing customer tastes and preferences.

My own experience tells me that there will always be market disruptions caused by innovation, however, I'm also certain that we are not likely to see the same type of seismic shifts in technology that we have seen in the past. Unfortunately, it would seem that many vendors have failed to recognize that the old days of explosive year-on-year growth are over.

SO WHAT? A common by-product of a mature market is increased competition and this has gradually led to an oversupply of vendors. Customers are now much better educated about IT products and services than at any other point in history meaning that the traditional role of the vendor sales person has changed dramatically. Sales leaders are now facing some new challenges that will require a radical rethink on almost all aspects of their field sales execution plans.

Vendor Consolidation

Another typical by-product of industry maturity is vendor rationalization and consolidation. The current oversupply of vendors means that customers are looking to identify means by which they can reduce the number of vendors that are required to run their businesses. As a result, an increasing number of IT vendors are identifying significant synergies and business benefits through mergers and acquisitions (M&A). IT M&A spending hit a post-GFC record of nearly a quarter-trillion dollars in 2013, driven by a series of major take-privates and large-scale industry consolidation *(451 Research, 2014)*.

The age of the 'super-vendor' has now also arrived as the large established global vendors (such as HP, IBM, and Oracle etc.) continue to add to their vast portfolios via inorganic growth strategies. In part, this surge in M&A activity is being driven by the vendors' desperate need to continue to identify growth opportunities (primarily to satisfy their equity owning stakeholders) and to remain relevant in the eyes of their customers. However, this explosion in M&A activity is also being driven by the increasingly important customer requirement of *doing more business with less vendors.* For some vendors, the strategy seems to be mostly about being able to take more and more products to their existing installed base of customers. For other vendors, it is more about finding technology acquisitions that enable them to participate in growth markets, and to plot a path from highly competitive established markets to more monopolistic market outcomes.

IBM recently paid USD$2billon to purchase public *cloud* services provider, *SoftLayer Technologies*, looking to narrow the gap with *Amazon Web Services. Salesforce.com,* more than doubled its cumulative M&A spending with its big step into marketing automation software. Salesforce.com paid $2.5bn for *ExactTarget*, the single largest transaction in the sector in 2013 *(451 Research).*

According to PwC, some of the key drivers of future growth in M&A activity are the (now) usual suspects –software-as-a-service (SaaS), mobile devices, analytics and *big data* applications – while the historical standard bearers of the industry (PCs and IT services) continue to slow *(PwC, 2013)*.

These current trends in vendor consolidation are now also creating an increase in the number of large slow-moving multi-product *super*-vendors, some of whom are either unwilling or unable to acknowledge the changes that are now taking place within their customer marketplaces. These same legacy *super*-vendors with their multiple lines of business continue to grapple with an integrated approach to customer engagement and all of this is now challenging the legacy sales models for vendors.

SO WHAT? The current oversupply of vendors means that customers are now actively seeking to identify means by which they can to do **"more business with less vendors"**. Some IT vendors are now forced to consider inorganic growth options (M&A) simply to remain competitive and relevant with their customers. Large multiproduct vendors are often slow to react to market changes making it difficult for sales leaders who must ensure coordinated customer engagement across multiple lines of business.

The Cloud and 'everything-as-a-service'

The information technology infrastructure of the world is swiftly being transformed by the emergence of cloud computing (*cloud*)—that is, the delivery of IT and business processes as digital services. As one of the key technology enablers in this current shift to the customer-led economy, *cloud* is now finally playing an important role in changing the way that businesses identify, acquire, and consume IT products and services. According to a recent (2015) report published by PwC, *agility* is now cited by 78% of CIOs as the main reason for *cloud* investment – to respond rapidly to changing business needs – rating above scalability, cost reduction and innovation.

KEY

Up until a couple of years ago, the *cloud* was primarily a concept for IT infrastructure solutions delivered *'as-a-service'*. Whilst the term still confuses people, in 2015 *cloud* is no longer simply an IT infrastructure play. According to IDC, cloud-delivery is now *business as usual*, and by 2016, *cloud* will be just another delivery model for a range of *"everything as-a-service'* (or *'XaaS'*) offerings that are based on infrastructure-as-a-service (IaaS), platform-as-a-service (PaaS), and software-as-a-service (SaaS).

'XaaS' facilitates business agility and cost efficiencies through *'pay-as-you-go'* models and this commercial benefit alone is now dramatically changing the business models for many IT vendors.

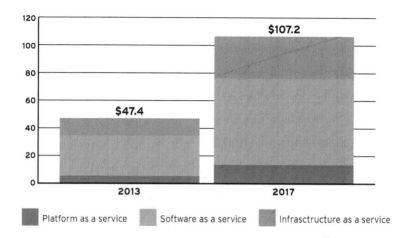

Some industry experts are now saying that there is evidence that *cloud* services are beginning to move into a *"Chapter Two"* phase where the scale of *cloud* adoption will not only be much larger, but also more user and solution driven. In this phase of growth, *cloud* and the other *technology megatrends* – mobile, social, and *Big Data* – will become even more interdependent as they continue to drive growth and innovation across all industries that depend on IT *(IDC, 2014)*. Worldwide spending on public IT *cloud* services will reach $47.4 billion in 2014 and is expected to be more than $107 billion in 2017, according to a new forecast from IDC. Over the 2014 –2017 forecast period, public IT *cloud* services will have a compound annual growth rate (CAGR) of 23.5%, five times that of the IT industry as a whole *(IDC, 2014)*.

According to Raj Mudaliar (senior analyst of the IT services research group at IDC Australia), "in responding to these changes over the next five years, IT services providers (vendors) will increasingly have to change their business models to mimic those of pure-play *cloud* providers by making strategic investments," *(IDC, 2014)*.

As important as *cloud* has now become, its economic significance is often misunderstood. That lies less in the technology, which is relatively straightforward, than in the new business models the cloud will enable. As a traditional incumbent vendor, IBM appears to be leading the charge in embracing enterprise *cloud*, a position that they have enhanced through investments of $7 billion on approximately 15 acquisitions in recent times, most notably SoftLayer in 2013.

> **SO WHAT?** *Cloud*-based models are now facilitating major changes in buyer preferences which vendors must urgently acknowledge and address. *Cloud* platforms help to facilitate *consumption-based* models where customers pay vendors only according to actual resources used (as utility providers have always done), and this is now a major 'game changer' for high tech vendors. Established vendors will increasingly have to revise their entire business models and delivery capabilities to mimic those of pure-play *cloud* providers and MSPs.

Transition to 'Managed Services'

At a macro-economic level, developed economies usually derive very high proportions of gross domestic product (GDP) from the services sector. 'Services' is a significant part of the Australian economy representing about 70 per cent of Australia's GDP and employing four out of five Australians (*DFAT, 2014*). The standard industry lifecycle model typically dealt with manufactured goods, but today's developed economies are now heavily skewed towards *services*, as a natural extension of declining product-based models. The advent of the internet alone is transforming many business models from "things" to people and services (*Investopedia.com 2014*). Whilst this definition of services relates to a wide range of products, there is also a clear trend towards the consumption of *service-based* IT products. Managed Service Provision (MSP) continues to grow rapidly as more businesses realize that purchasing IT functions *"as-a-service"* no longer means losing control over critical business functions (*AGC Research, 2009*).

Why is this trend important? Because customers can now demand new pricing models and this is a large departure from years gone by when vendors could set whatever business, pricing and delivery models suited them. Well-trained and well-informed professional buyers are now looking to vendors for new and innovative products and business models that better reflect their evolving needs and actual usage. MSPs and *consumption-based* pricing models mean that customers are able to transition certain software applications to *'subscription'* or *'rental-based'* licensing models – taking these software expenses out of capital expenditure (CAPEX) and into operational expenditure (OPEX). Buying IT products "as-a-service" is certainly not a new concept, but customers are now adopting these new models at a rapid rate. *Consumption-based* pricing models are now highly attractive to IT buyers. It is much more cost effective for IT buyers to embrace managed services than it is to build new data centers and then try to find new highly-skilled staff to manage them.

The rise and rise of *Salesforce.com* is a prime example of how buyer behaviour is trending away from owning products, and towards *renting* services bundled up as products. *Salesforce.com*, a *cloud* computing company, provides customer relationship management (CRM) products to businesses. It offers a technology platform for internet-based computing, storage, and connectivity solutions for customers and developers. Salesforce's rapid growth is now being fueled increasingly by large deals for its *cloud* software, according to its CEO Marc Benioff (*CiteWorld, 2013*). Cloud-based delivery or managed service provision will continue to drive *consumption-based* pricing and rapid growth in the use of externally sourced services.

> **SO WHAT?** Customers no longer have to accept the legacy vendor models of the past where customers invest large sums up-front in the hope that the vendor's product will create the value that the vendor had promised. Indeed, customers no longer need to assume all of the risk, and vendors' sales departments are now being forced to change their business models.

IT Outsourcing (ITO)

In conjunction with the transition to managed services, the practice of seeking external resources to provide part (or in some cases, all) of an organisation's IT function has been around for a long time. Outsourcing IT brings with it many benefits, and these benefits are increasingly attractive for businesses that require competitive advantages beyond simple cost optimization. Outsourcing selected functions to expert partners allows businesses to focus on core competencies whilst also lowering costs.

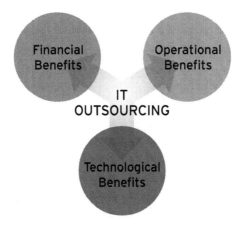

Of course, outsourcing is definitely not new and, as trends in this area have waxed and waned over the years, today's businesses continue to grapple with the on-going scarcity of skilled resources to facilitate the management of complex IT infrastructure. Coupled with the skills shortage, the trend is now moving rapidly towards 'XaaS' meaning that the outlook for ITO growth appears positive. The growth rate of 'XaaS' will necessarily dictate that more and more IT components will effectively become outsourced (CIO Magazine, 2012).

CIOs are now stating that business agility is critical and will require that they have the means of ensuring that their business can provision services more quickly and, importantly, pay for just the services they utilize (IDC, 2014). This continued pressure on CIOs to lower costs and adjust service requirements more quickly plays directly into the hands of the managed services and ITO providers.

SO WHAT? Businesses are being driven to become more **agile**, and managed service provision along with IT outsourcing will undoubtedly increase into the future. Vendor sales organisations must be clear about how this trend impacts their value proposition and the extent to which it also creates opportunities and threats.

Centralized Strategic Sourcing

In 2015, everyone knows that the internet has created a level playing field – more or less. The practice of sourcing goods and services from global markets across geographic boundaries is not a new concept, however, with continued technology advancements, IT buyers in today's globalized economies are now taking a more systematic and holistic approach to engagement with all of their suppliers. Strategic sourcing, procurement and vendor management functions within many businesses now account for an increasingly large proportion of the annual business spend and global procurement strategies can now create significant savings for multi-national corporations (MNCs) who can negotiate favorable global pricing structures and terms with their suppliers regardless of location. National pricing models and country-specific licensing have previously favored vendors, and customers no longer need to accept these restrictions. As an example, software licensing is no longer a country-by-country sales model. Multinational corporations can now leverage their market position better than ever before to negotiate international transfer rights which allow a centralized management function or "floating pool" of licenses to be utilized on an as needs basis.

Every MNC now has some form of centralized procurement functions, particularly for big ticket items such as IT. These procurement functions are increasingly integrated to optimize and leverage economies of scale, and to minimize the *rogue purchasing* that so often creates duplication and waste in many large enterprises. However, the current reality is that very few IT vendors have successfully implemented an effective program for the on-going management of global customer requirements. Those vendor sales organisations with global reach are reorienting their sales efforts to better service their largest MNC customers, and this trend is going to increase dramatically as globalization, commoditization and online purchasing removes borders and creates a more level playing field for IT buyers.

Global Customer Supplier Relationship

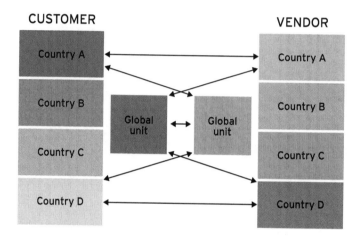

SO WHAT? A natural consequence of strategic sourcing or any centralized procurement function is supplier rationalization. The commercial benefits that can be derived from supplier rationalization continues to force technology buyers to search for new ways of **doing more business with less vendors.**
Vendor sales people must now become much more proficient at providing large MNC customers with a coordinated and systematic approach to doing business.

CHAPTER 2

The Buying Journey

Vendors no longer participate in the entire buying journey

Customers generally progress through three broad stages of the customers' buying cycle (a clearly outdated term that has now somehow morphed into *'buying journey')*: Awareness-Consideration-Purchase. Sophisticated buyers often use much more detailed processes and workflows to ensure integrity for each step of the *buying journey*. In the same way that vendors will regularly create a bid-team for a large sales opportunities, customers now often create project teams to manage the procurement of *big ticket-long cycle* purchases. Every customer has a variation of the steps and gateways that span the *buying journey* (as outlined in the diagram below) and one of the challenges for sales people has always been to ensure that they have a complete understanding of the idiosyncrasies of each customer's approach, and unique steps, of the *buying journey*.

Typical Buying Journey

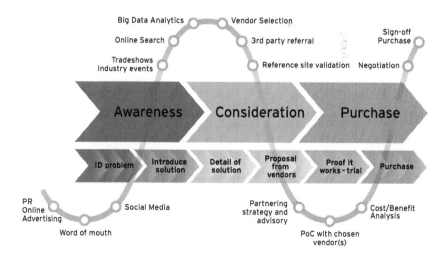

The sales cycle (or various activities that make up a typical sale) has always run in parallel with the *buying journey*, and savvy sales people have always understood and leveraged this connection to ensure success.

Buying Journey and Sales Cycle

Throughout the early stages of the IT industry, businesses relied heavily on the specialist (and very scarce) IT knowledge and expertise of their vendors. In fact, businesses often had very little access to IT knowledge other than via their vendors and, as a natural consequence of this knowledge gap, vendors held the power and were often viewed as *'trusted advisors'* in almost every customer business. As discussed earlier, times have changed to the point that customers now have access to vast amounts of knowledge and information via a multitude of sources, and they also have developed specialist in-house skill-sets capable of providing the knowledge and guidance that their vendors were once relied upon to provide.

Vendor (SUSE): "These days, customers need not rely on us to educate them in new technologies and trends…instead, customers are doing their own research and driving their own strategies without the assistance and influence of the vendor. This makes it much more difficult for us (vendor) to engage and influence the customer during the sales cycle. In fact, the cycle has shortened in that it now begins when the customer has their requirements and is ready to hear 'our best and final pitch'. We're engaging later which means it's harder to influence and win deals."

A recent study (by Corporate Board Executive) of more than 1,400 B2B customers found that customers now complete, *"on average, nearly 60% of the typical purchasing decision – researching solutions, ranking options, setting requirements, benchmarking pricing and so on – before even having a conversation with a vendor."* Further supporting this is another study done by *Prelytix*, which states that *"buyers are engaging vendors only after having completed 60–65%% of their decision-making process"*.

Vendor involvement in the new buying journey

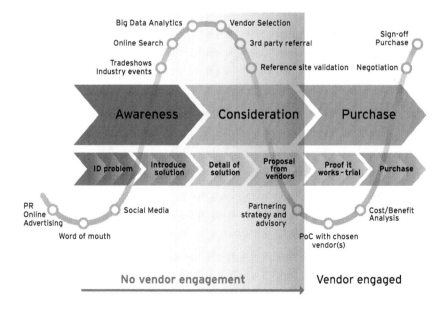

Ms Diane Fernly-Jones is the ex-CIO of an Australian based company – Leighton Holdings. Diane has many years of experience in dealing directly with a multitude of IT vendors, and recently stated: *"My team and I would do all the preliminary work ourselves or use an independent third party. We usually have a good knowledge of the market through our existing senior staff and technical experts. There are a lot of research sources (Gartner et al) and independent advisors available to avoid being swamped by vendor sales people, whose only role is to sell their product...we need to be very clear about our needs so we buy the right product to do the job."*

So, depending on which research you subscribe to, it's now clear that vendor sales people no longer influence the *buying journey* as they once did and, in my view, this is possibly the most significant change to impact B2B sales in more than 100 years. This is evidence that we have moved from a *vendor-push* model to a *customer-pull* model where the vendor sales person now has much less control, and this is a major game changer for sales people.

> **SO WHAT?** The buying journey has changed. Customers now deliberately engage vendors very late in the **buying journey** which dramatically reduces the role of the vendor sales person. Being called into a sales opportunity late creates risk for vendors and limits their ability to influence the sale. Vendor sales people are now wasting significant amounts of company resource when they fail to adequately qualify exactly where they are within their customer's new buying journey.

CHAPTER 3

Oversupply of Vendors

We need to do more business with less vendors

When I first began selling software B2B (circa 1996), practically every aspect of the IT world was complex. Back then, customers would seek guidance from vendors and would rapidly embrace solutions that could give them a competitive advantage regardless of the degrees of complexity involved. These same customers would happily find any means by which they could to cobble together solutions across disparate platforms with little regard for the increasingly complex environments that they were creating. What resulted for the customer was a veritable patchwork quilt of semi-temporary IT platforms and applications all connected via highly bespoke and custom-built systems and networks. Strangely, during this time, CIOs would almost wear this 'complexity' of their highly unique custom-built IT environment as some sort of badge of honor.

From this complexity grew a massive list of IT suppliers each of whom was responsible for their small part in the overall IT ecosystem for each customer. Customers would openly admit to preferring to deal with specialist vendors rather than multi-product generalist vendors simply because they were all chasing a "best-of-breed" outcome. With hindsight, it is now easy to see how this unplanned and mostly ad hoc approach to highly custom-built environments would ultimately result in some limitations and long term disadvantages for businesses that need to increasingly respond to change. Now, two decades later, complexity is the sworn enemy of CIOs who prefer standardized solutions, from smaller numbers of vendors, which can be switched on/off as business needs flex and change. Simplification increases agility by reducing system interdependence which then facilitates faster time-to-market.

Each of the Australian vendor management personnel that were interviewed as part of this book all agreed strongly with the notion that doing *"more business with less vendors"* was no longer just some sort of industry catch phrase. The time has now come for IT buyers to actually reduce the cost of doing business and one obvious way to achieve this is simply by being smarter about how many vendors are actually required to run their business operations. Vendor rationalization is now in full swing across most businesses today with all interviewees stating that their objective is to actively reduce the total number of existing ("on panel") vendors.

> Customer (Suncorp): "We are looking to the multi-product vendors to displace the smaller single-product vendors because engaging with the small vendors for a single product is not cost effective."

> Customer (NAB): "A large number of our vendors sell us one product or service, and that is normally not cost effective, nor does it fit within our risk guidelines. Big companies like NAB can be slow to pay and, for small vendors, this can sometimes mean life or death. Thus, we avoid dealing with small vendors that only sell us one product wherever possible. We always aim to protect the bank by ensuring that the source code (for software) provided by a small vendor is kept in escrow in case the vendor's business fails."

It is not uncommon these days to see companies consolidating vendor contracts down to one vendor in specific areas or across the board to gain volume pricing discounts and to cut out the costs of dealing with dozens of suppliers (TechTarget, 2010).

Thrifty IT buyers are also taking full advantage of the myriad of eProcurement and online purchasing services in particular for low complexity and standard transactional purchases. This multichannel approach to aggregated purchasing can dramatically lower acquisition costs for buyers across almost every industry. Even global car makers such as GM now offer online purchase options for cars. This evolution is partly based around removing the need to engage directly with vendor sales teams where it's deemed not necessary, thus minimizing the overall cost in dealing with vast numbers of vendors. Engaging with, in some cases, hundreds of sales people, each wanting to engage in regular meetings, is a significant cost factor for businesses, not to mention the enormous amount of time (and cost) required at the backend with contracts and licensing agreements.

> **SO WHAT?** If customers need to **"do more business with less vendors"**, then some vendors will be winners and some will be losers. Well established multi-product vendors will be able to increase their footprint within an existing account, however this will normally be at the expense of another vendor. Vendors that are low on their customer's **'vendor stack'** (see Chapter 4) are now at risk of being 'culled' from the account. Single product vendors face enormous challenges moving forwards.

online procurement tool (empowering the customer)
customer-pull model ... consumption model;
where a customer can increase or decrease uses
based off their needs/requirements - KEY point
is agility.

The Vendor Stack

Businesses can no longer afford to engage with so many vendors

Virtually every business has some means by which to rank-order its suppliers-vendors in terms of strategic importance or level of priority. Businesses now pay increasing attention to what is referred to as the 'vendor stack' and the myriad of costs associated with vendor and contract management. Quite often the 'vendor stack' (or vendor ranking) is based around some notion of annual spend with each vendor whilst, in other cases, vendors are ranked according to how critical their product or service is to on-going business operations and technology ecosystem. Regardless of which method is used, the fact is that all buyers of IT products and services place their vendors into a rank-order of some sort.

Typical vendor stack

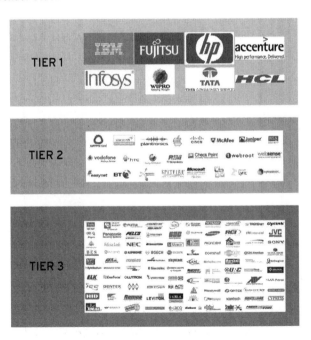

Note: Vendor logos were randomly chosen for illustrative purposes only.

National Australia Bank (NAB) broadly categorizes its enormous quantity of IT suppliers into three broad Tiers. Tier 1 represents those suppliers that are the most strategic and critical to bank operations. NAB refers to these five Tier 1 vendors as 'prime' vendors. At the time of the writing of this book, NAB also has thirty-one Tier 2 vendors and then there are approximately 1,100 Tier 3 vendors spanning all bank operations and lines of business. Importantly, NAB has stated an aim to reduce the quantity of Tier 3 vendors by around 50% – back to a more manageable and cost effective number of approximately 550 – 600.

NAB 'vendor stack' (as at December, 2013)

Vendor Stack	Number of Vendors
Tier 1	5
Tier 2	31
Tier 3	1,100

NAB is aiming to "halve" its total number of Tier 3 vendors

According to Prue Jacobson (former Head of Technology Procurement & Supplier Management), Qantas also broadly categorizes its vendors into 3 Tiers. Prue also highlighted the approximate percentage of annual spend attributable to each Tier of the Qantas 'vendor stack' (see table below):

Qantas 'vendor stack' (as at August, 2013)

Vendor Stack	Number of Vendors	% of total annual IT Spend
Tier 1	9	86%
Tier 2	13	7%
Tier 3	363	7%

Qantas aims to reduce Tier 3 vendors back to circa 100

Although vendor ranking is certainly not a new concept, the current trend is that customers are now desperately searching for ways to reduce the vast numbers of vendors that supply their businesses. Low priority vendors now face being *culled* from their customer's *vendor stack* often because there are simply too many vendors supplying most businesses.

The next important trend here is that customers are increasingly relying on a smaller number of multi-product or 'prime' suppliers to provide the vast majority of the technology products and services that they require to run their businesses. In the case of Qantas, 86% of the entire annual spend on IT is currently channeled through only nine Tier 1 ('prime') vendors, rendering all Tier 2 and 3 vendors insignificant by comparison. The implication here is that vendors currently ranked in the Tier 3 category, or new vendors currently not supplying, may well be forced to sell their products and services to Qantas through a Tier 1 or Tier 2 vendor who has multi-vendor engagement capability.

> Customer (Qantas): "We can no longer justify the time required to engage with a Tier 3 vendor, and will be looking to redirect Tier 3 vendors to engage via a prime (Tier 1) vendor."

Tier 3 vendors may have to sell via a Tier 1 ('prime') vendor

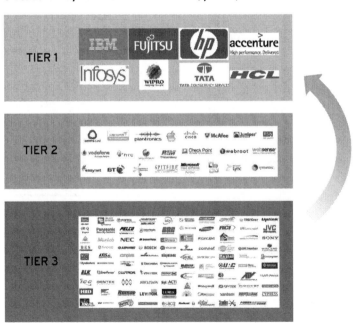

Note: Vendor logos were randomly chosen for illustrative purposes only.

This point above has significant implications for vendor sales leaders due mostly to the dramatic change that it will cause in their engagement models and go-to-market plans if they are indeed forced to push their products to their end user via a Tier 1 or 'prime' partner. Anyone that has experienced selling via a channel partner knows that it's a vastly different model which often means that the vendor has very little control over most aspects of the sales cycle. One of the most critical implications in all of this is that many of the world-best vendors right now have sales personnel 'spinning their wheels' within target accounts that they will never be permitted to sell to (more on this later).

There are many vendor sales leaders currently operating that are apparently unaware of where they are categorized within the 'vendor stack' for each of their customers. Research into this topic has highlighted a surprising fact that a large percentage of vendor sales people simply never ask their customers the all-important question about where they rank on their customer's 'vendor stack. *n vendor tiers)*

> Vendor (SUSE) – "Almost none of our sales people ask this question nor would they probably understand the importance of the answer".

As a consequence of this current trend towards vendor rationalization, sales people will no longer be able to avoid the investment required in developing closer customer relationships. The old model whereby sales people would simply hand everything over to 'support' once the purchase order has been received (moving quickly onto the next sale) will no longer be acceptable to customers that want to wring every last piece of value they can from each purchase. Customers now, quite rightly, demand a more 'arms around' experience from their vendors, and sales people will be required to spend more time than ever ensuring deep and ongoing customer satisfaction.

> Vendor (Experian) – "Whilst you must build a good relationship with the procurement personnel, it's important to move up the strategic vendor curve by developing relationships across the business, and becoming deeply embedded into your customers' businesses."

Strategic alliance partnerships, which in my experience are often a waste of time and resource, are now being brought back into clear focus. Vendor sales leaders must now allocate more time into building a systematic approach to relationships with other IT vendors that can provide a pathway into a target account. *'Buddying up'* with Tier 1 partners within each customer account will help remove some of the risks of being culled whilst simultaneously assisting vendor sales people to better understand what's happening in each account and where competitive threats may exist.

Vendors whose ambition it is to identify and sell into 'net-new' customers or *green-field* target segments can no longer simply rely on the old *'knocking on doors'* approach. This traditional approach to prospecting for new business sales now has the potential to waste significant amounts of the vendor resource if the sales person is unaware of the *vendor stack* implications outlined above. This will be discussed in more detail on page 65 – Cold Calling.

The implications for new or "start-up" vendors are even more dramatic. Brand new vendors that now attempt to sell into the enterprise customer market (in Australia) will also face significant headwinds if they attempt the traditional sales approach. These newly-established vendors will fail miserably unless they can quickly establish some very important relationships with the right alliance partners. Not only will this approach take longer but it will also will likely be a much more complex and costly sales cycle. Selling via an IBM or a HP is a very different *go-to-market* model from selling directly to an end-user.

> **SO WHAT?** The vast majority of vendors have failed to recognize that they may now be at risk of being culled from their customers **vendor stack**. Vendor rationalization is gaining speed, and some Tier 2 and Tier 3 and vendors will have to align themselves with Tier 1 or 'prime' vendors as the channel to the end-user as part of the customer retention strategy. Vendor sales people must urgently find out where they rank on their customer's **vendor stack**.

CHAPTER 5

Off-Panel Purchasing

IT buyers can no longer afford to engage with new vendors

It is now common for enterprise level organisations – corporate and government – to have what is referred to as a *locked down* Approved IT Supplier List, meaning that they will not accept new vendors. Having an extensive supplier list normally requires careful (and very costly) management of tens of thousands of contracts, and individual product licensing agreements each year. Software Asset Management (*SAM*) alone is now a major cost in managing today's business operations, and the on-going search for more efficient means of sourcing and procuring IT products has meant that many customers (small, medium and large) are now re-engineering their entire vendor engagement and management processes to take advantage of technologies that can help them lower the cost of doing business with such a vast number of vendors.

As a result of this new focus on the increasing cost of vendor management, many enterprises are now in the process of *trimming* back their extensive supplier lists, or simply ensuring that they only deal with vendors that can provide a multi-product engagement. This has important implications for any vendor categorized as Tier 3 (or higher), and also any new vendors seeking to do business with an enterprise level customer. In many cases, the purchase of IT products that are to be made '*off-panel*' will attract enormous internal scrutiny and will likely require all manner of business case justification before approval will be granted to engage with a new vendor. The implication here is that if a vendor is not currently doing business with a particular target customer, then it is highly likely that they may never be granted a '*seat at the table*'.

Imagine, if you will, the amount of time and money that could be wasted by a vendor sales person in the attempt to engage, qualify and sell to a new customer account only to find out (at the 11th hour, or the final stage of the sales cycle) that the customer *"cannot engage with your company directly because we are not permitted to deal with any new vendors"*. Having experienced this first hand, I know that this is now a regular occurrence with inexperienced, or should I say, poorly coached, vendor sales people.

Customer (Qantas): "Unless a vendor comes highly recommended, and can quickly demonstrate a) a clear link with our strategy, and b) a clear competitive advantage for us, then we won't bother engaging. We have a matrix that looks at a range of metrics for vendor suitability and, although we need to improve the rigor of our gateways, we will always look to find a comparable solution from an existing supplier. Alternative is that the 'new' vendor engages through one of our Tier 1 or Tier 2 vendors."

Customer (NAB): "More and more of our vendors will be asked to engage through a 'prime' Tier 1 vendor in the future. The role of the 'prime' is partly risk mitigation – we hate dealing with small vendors who may be here today and gone tomorrow."

Customer (Suncorp): "Dealing with so many vendors is a massive cost for us – we have just dropped 450 people out of our own internal IT departments. We need fewer people as we move towards cloud – self-service – offerings which leverages less vendors. Ultimately we are moving to having less vendors anyway, and whilst we can engage with new vendors, there is a major gateway there. No vendor can get through the gate without a solid internal business case justification. If it's just a reseller, then that's easy. We have made it really difficult for any business unit to engage 'off panel' and this has been done through creating 'blocker' programs that prevent off panel purchases – this program will stop the on-going proliferation of new IT vendors."

SO WHAT? Many enterprise level businesses now refuse to engage directly with any vendor that is not already on the existing supplier list. New 'off-panel' vendors will likely be required to engage via a Tier 1 (**'prime'**) vendor.

Selling via a *'prime'* partner is a totally different sales execution plan from selling direct into customer accounts, and this type of sale requires a different set of skills and resources, along with a new commercial and pricing model. Vendor sales leaders must acknowledge this risk and rethink their sales execution plans.

CHAPTER 6

Cost Optimization

IT buyers are now more focused than ever on
driving costs down

Today's business are trying desperately to rein in costs, and IT spend, which is now a major cost centre for most businesses, is being scrutinized more than ever before. The annual spend on IT-related services is now the single largest component of annual outgoings for many organisations, and CEOs and CIOs are looking more closely than ever before and how they can reduce the annual IT spend. According to Gartner, 70% of enterprises will have the potential to reduce IT costs by 25% or more *(Gartner, 2014)*

> Customer (Qantas): *"Supplier relationship management was recently raised as a major cost for our enterprise level businesses."*

> Customer (Qantas): *"Agility is vitally important in our industry – if we find a vendor that can give us a quick win that translates to a competitive advantage then we will be more inclined to work with that new vendor. Time-to-value and speed-of-deployment is everything nowadays."*

The first place that many CIOs look to make savings is through the improved vendor management and the renegotiation of IT service and maintenance contracts with their vendors. Also underway are efforts to consolidate vendor contracts and software licenses across business units to get better pricing and eliminate contract redundancies. In other cases, enterprises are opting to eliminate aspects of their contracts completely whilst outsourcing wherever possible *(TechTarget Report, 2010)*.

In 2015, many businesses still face the issue of decentralized purchasing whereby business units often purchase their own IT products, which usually leads to the enterprise missing out on the much-needed economies of scale and volume license discounts. CIOs increasingly look to eliminate this *'rogue purchasing'* by switching a licensing contract from the business-unit level to a corporate level to realize greater buying power and better discounts.

In the context of what is now a highly competitive globalized IT market, it is often the smaller, hungrier vendors that are willing to offer price breaks that will sway enterprises away from incumbent vendors. Moreover, as customers continue to demand more flexibility and *risk share* from vendors, the winners will be those vendors that are agile and can quickly adapt their business models to meet these changing customer demands.

Important

> Customer (NAB): "You can often save money with the smaller vendors because they're more concerned about building a long term relationship with you, but then you have to balance the risks associated with that vendor going out of business because there is no profit left in the deal for them."

SO WHAT? IT spend is being scrutinized more now than ever before and many enterprise level business are now refusing to engage directly with any vendor that is not already an existing supplier. Whilst customers are now desperately trying to reduce costs, vendor's sales people are still charged with continuously delivering increasing revenues from each customer. Vendor sales people are now more diametrically opposed from their customers than ever before. There are tough times ahead for vendor sales people.

CHAPTER 7

Consumption-based models

Cloud computing enables consumption-based pricing models

Consumption-based licensing is a relatively new term which describes the concept that allows a customer to utilize fluctuating quantities of a product (mostly software) on a monthly or quarterly basis as the needs of the business flex up and down. This new approach is anathema to traditional vendors and it stems from the increasing customer demands to allow better utilization and flexibility around paying the vendor only for what is used. Naturally, many traditional vendors would prefer the old legacy perpetual license models where the customer pays for a full license fee (up-front), regardless of the future levels of intended or actual usage. From my own experience, I can assert that these old models, where the balance is all in favor of the vendor, will cease to exist within the next 3–5 years. Consumption-based models are not only fairer, but they also provide customers with the flexibility to rapidly alter course as their business changes dictate.

> Vendor (ScienceLogic): "There is most definitely a drive towards subscription models, especially with our service provider customers. As a relatively new vendor, we are more able to align with new buying methods and new models. Around 65% of our customers are moving (or have moved) to our subscription based pricing models."

> Vendor (SUSE): "Rather than traditional perpetual software licensing, customers are starting to request subscription based licensing. Everyone is trying to minimize capital expenditure with smarter more flexible licensing models."

With the emergence of *managed service provision* and cloud computing comes opportunities for businesses – large and small – to leverage new business models and turn capital infrastructure expenses into variable costs. Reducing operating leverage has long been a goal of corporate management and *'everything-as-a-service'* now allows businesses to purchase the exact quantity of resources as and when they require them – increasing efficiencies and improving productivity, by effectively switching services on/off as the business requirements change.

> Customer (NAB): "We see cloud as a big disruptor with things like infrastructure on demand which has been something that we have been striving to achieve for a long time."

> Customer (Suncorp): "Cloud computing allows us to drive cost out of our business. Vendors have to put a new hat on – for example, NetApp saw their market eroding, and partnered with the big cloud providers."

> Customer (Westpac): "Cloud is having a major impact, but it's not a wholesale change for the bank. We are simply cherry picking applications on a case-by-case basis."

> Customer (Qantas): "Cloud is absolutely changing our business – but it's not all just about commercial benefits, although they are important. You must begin with the customer outcome – that is, will this solution give our customers a better experience?"

All businesses are striving for that optimal point of leverage where sales can be maximized in times of economic growth, and where risks can be minimized in times of economic turbulence. For example, outsourcing has always been regarded as a method used to change the ratio of fixed costs to variable costs in a business, and also by making variable costs more predictable. Similarly, acquiring IT products as "services" through a managed service provider (MSP) or *cloud* provider is regarded by many as a form of outsourcing which also reduces the reliance on high capital expense items, thus reducing operating leverage and risk to the business.

All the expenses incurred through *cloud* or MSP services can typically be written-off in the same year for tax purposes; whereas large IT equipment purchase have to be capitalized and written-off over number of years. This transition to consumption-based models is now beginning to have a major impact on the bottom line of many customer businesses, and shareholders are the ultimate winners with the likelihood of higher returns and reduced business risk.

With all of that said, *cloud* computing does not impact all vendors. Some vendors do not believe that their products are likely to ever be made available via *cloud-based* delivery. Certain technologies, such as security or 'database' technologies, will always remain *'on-premises'* and managed by in-house staff. The business risks associated with these technologies being hosted off-premise will keep certain technologies within the *firewall*. That's not to say that these vendors will not be dragged along by the ever-increasing customer demands for more flexibility and fairer *consumption-based* pricing models.

> **SO WHAT?** **Cloud** computing facilitates **consumption-based** pricing models which are not only fairer, but much more flexible than legacy vendor business models. Customers will increasingly demand these models from vendors and this will undoubtedly impact vendor profitability and short term revenue results. Vendor sales leaders must redefine their business models to allow for this mega-trend.

CHAPTER 8

Engagement Models

IT buyers now have greater leverage than ever before

As outlined in previous chapters, the balance of power has now shifted from vendors to customers, and we are now seeing a new era where the highly sought after customers call the shots – especially at the 'enterprise' end of town. This is a big turnaround from when I first began my career in IT sales when vendor innovation was responsible for driving the markets. Nowadays, it is the increasing power of educated IT buyers that has the leverage to insist that vendors provide them with a greater value-add. This now comes in the form of a high touch, *'arms around'* experience, and vendors that fail to offer their customers these improved levels of handling and attention will be increasingly outperformed by those vendors that are prepared to listen to their customers and make the necessary changes.

> Customer (Westpac): "IBM and vendors of that ilk spend USD $4–5Billion on R&D for new products – how much do they spend on innovating their sales approach? Why don't they spend more time and money listening to what their customers actually want, and then change their models to suit? We want more flexible usage-based models – not the old legacy models that no longer work for us. Happy to commit to longer terms, as long as we have flexibility – a smorgasbord – all you can eat – take value out of the "committed software stack" meaning that we can switch on/off the products and services that we need at any point without penalty."

Vendors are now required to constantly improve the way in which each and every transaction is managed – both *pre* and *post*-sale. Whether vendors like it or not, IT buyers can now demand increasingly higher levels of service and value-add from each of their vendors at every step along the new *buying journey*. Some vendors are aware of this with many now paying greater attention to measuring customer satisfaction, however it is my opinion that a large percentage of the vendors operating today remain wedded to their legacy *modus operandi* which requires the sales person to foster a *'churn and burn'* mentality.

> *Customer (Westpac): "We suggested to IBM that we want to separate the vendor sales personnel from the on-going support personnel. We know that sales guys are driven by sales revenue, thus we suggested that the vendor allocate us with 'deployment managers' whose sole purpose is to simply to keep us happy and to keep the product/service moving – essentially build trust. This is exactly what we do in our business with the Customer Relationship Managers that service our customers post sale."*

Put simply, customers are no longer required to submit to vendor *"lock in"* when there are so many alternative or substitute products now available. Nor are customers willing to continue to buy into models that require them to assume all the risk. Vendors that do not begin to listen to their customers and take a longer term view of the relationship will face a future outlook that is based around negative growth and declining revenues.

SO WHAT? Vendors no longer have the power. The rising focus on customer satisfaction measurements such as **Net Promoter Score (NPS)** is reflective of a shift whereby customers can now demand a greatly improved 'service' from each vendor. MSP and **cloud** offerings can be easily switched on and off meaning customers are no longer 'locked in' to a particular vendor. Thus, vendor sales leaders must ensure that they have the right customer engagement models in place that can produce positive customer perception.

CHAPTER 9

Risk Sharing

More vendor flexibility is now required

Businesses must become more agile than ever before in order to compete in these modern times. As discussed in the previous chapter, customers are no longer willing to accept the legacy license models that are the preference of vendors and are instead now increasingly demanding that vendors offer new *consumption-based* models.

> Customer (NAB): *"Very few vendors truly understand, or can provide, the types of models that we are looking for. Microsoft is one that is listening, and that has varied its old models to include enterprise subscription models such as Office 365."*

Vendors are now under pressure to move away from legacy pricing models (and the associated revenue streams) and re-think their commercial models in order to accommodate the growing number of IT buyers that are demanding increased flexibility. Whilst this transition may very well put downward pressure on vendor revenues in the short term, failure to offer increased flexibility to customers could have major implications for vendors.

Many of the traditional approaches to licensing IT products allowed the vendor to charge the customer the full amount up-front in return for a perpetual *'right to use'* the software. Most software vendors also offer annual maintenance and support which creates (in some cases) a lucrative annuity, or flow, revenue stream. Naturally, this type of model favors vendors, allowing full revenue capture and recognition up front, regardless of how often the customer actually utilizes the product in the future, or whether the product or service ever delivers the level of value that the vendor had promised during the *buying journey.*

Customers (IT buyers) have long argued that these legacy models do not fairly reflect their actual usage, nor do they provide any flexibility if user numbers vary inside the customer organisations. It is therefore hardly a surprise that IT buyers now demand more flexibility and a more equitable model that caters for actual usage and, whilst this will be a difficult bridge for vendors to cross, executive management of legacy vendors must transform their business models to allow customers greater commercial flexibility and improved delivery options.

> Vendor (ScienceLogic): "We are absolutely going to have to move towards consumption-based pricing. This will introduce operational and contractual challenges, and some vendors will prefer to maintain minimum commitment contracts; ultimately however, the industry will have to find a way."

> Vendor (Novell): "As an older heritage vendor, we acknowledge that customers want more flexible licensing options, however making changes to – in some cases – 30-year-old systems and processes is a major barrier for us. We will likely remain stuck with our legacy licensing models for some products, but will look to move to newer models wherever possible."

As competition among vendors intensifies, customer now expect their vendors to offer models that also involve some element of 'risk sharing' – particularly within the context of new products. In short, this usually means that vendors must now offer volume pricing discounts right up front at the beginning of a new relationship on the promise that volumes (and therefore vendor profitability) will increase as product adoption increases. Customers now expect their vendors to have some 'skin in the game' and to demonstrate genuine faith in their own product offerings by committing to a longer term relationship that ensures that maximum value can be extracted (by the customer) right throughout the product lifecycle.

> Customer (Qantas): – "We expect our vendors to put some skin in the game. Time-to-value and speed-of-deployment is everything nowadays."

It is virtually impossible to argue that vendors must provide their customers with more economic value-add than they have in the past and this now includes an increasing element of risk sharing.

SO WHAT? Customers can now demand more flexibility from vendors. Vendor business, pricing, and engagement models are now under the microscope as customers continue to leverage their new position of power.

Vendor sales leaders must become much more flexible and accommodating or face losing more sales than they win.

CHAPTER 10

Channels to Market

Strategic alliance partnerships are now back on the agenda

Strategic alliances or indirect channels to market will play an increasing role in the future for IT vendors. Selling to end-users via a third party or *'prime'* vendor is now more important than ever before. As discussed in previous chapters, vendor rationalization and the customer trend of moving away from direct engagement with smaller single product vendors is now gaining momentum. Every vendor interviewed as part of this research agreed that partnerships are always very difficult due to the conflicting interests of the respective sales organisations.

> *Vendor (SUSE) "Developing true alliance partnerships is becoming more important, yet most reps are too short– sighted, taking purchase orders direct so they can hit their individual monthly or quarterly quota. This type of action ends up damaging the partner relationships and making any sort of alliance partnership virtually impossible."*

Creating alliance partnerships is certainly not a new concept in the IT industry. However, a fresh approach to these engagements is now critical. Many vendors have previously wasted enormous amounts of time and money on strategic alliance relationships due mostly to unclear objectives and outcomes. Historically, these strategic alliance relationships have been more about hype than actual value creation. In order for these partnerships to actually create value, both parties must clarify the exact nature and purpose of the relationship, and new modes of incentive must be developed by vendors in order to gain genuine *'buy-in'* from their alliance partners.

Naturally, customers will usually engage on a more strategic and detailed basis with their Tier 1 or Tier 2 vendors, like IBM, HP or Fujitsu, and they will look to utilize these *big players* to help formulate a longer term strategy for their business road maps. In the case of Qantas, where circa

86% of the annual IT spend is channeled through their Tier 1 vendors, it makes sense on every level (commercial, strategic and operational) for Qantas to rely on their Tier 1 vendors to effectively aggregate (or sub-contract) multiple products from third party vendors – including some of their existing Tier 3 vendors. I believe that it will soon become the primary role of the smaller niche vendors to strategically align themselves with alliance partners or Tier 1 ('*prime*') vendors.

Sales compensation plans are designed to provide incentives and to reward certain behaviours, but rarely does a vendor compensation plan cater for the long term development of genuine partner alliances. Herein lies the issue: Sales people are driven by pressure to book as much revenue as possible each quarter/month, and this pressure creates the *tyranny of short-termism*. Rarely, if ever, will a vendor sales person commit the time required to develop an appropriate long term alliance partnership when these short term sales pressures loom large.

SO WHAT? Developing strategic alliance partnerships will become increasingly important for all vendors but this will come at a cost. Partnerships take time to develop and will be at the expense of short term revenue.

Vendor sales leaders will be forced to find ways to allocate already scarce resources to aligning themselves with strategic partners around key accounts as part of their customer retention strategy.

CHAPTER 11

The Case for Change

So what does all of the change outlined in previous chapters actually mean for vendor sales people? Surely sales people are dealing with change all the time? Haven't we seen this type of change before? Isn't this just natural market evolution? What's different about this round of changes? All pertinent questions, however the simple answer here is that never before have we seen such a dramatic change in the way that customers buy high tech products and services. Buyer behaviour has shifted so significantly that the traditional approach to selling complex products B2B is no longer compatible.

Let's back up for a moment. Most currently active sales people are oblivious to the fact that the B2B sales model that is most practiced today was actually designed in the 1880s – around 130 years ago. In 1884, Mr John H. Patterson bought a small but innovative cash register business – National Cash Register Company (NCR) – in Dayton, Ohio. This was at a time when the industrial revolution had spawned a new breed of businesses that could produce more products than they could sell and a new sales and distribution model was needed. NCR was at the forefront of this major change in business machines in the late nineteenth and early twentieth centuries and Patterson faced a major challenge in trying to sell what was at the time a complex product (cash registers) that few customers believed they needed. Patterson devised a bold and innovative sales model that would see him become known as *"the father of professional selling"*. Patterson created the B2B sales model that most vendor businesses still use to this day – 130 years later – and when you consider how times have changed since the 1880s, it beggars belief that Patterson's model is still being so widely used.

When you combine industry maturity with the fact that never before have IT buyers had access to the amount of information that they have today, then this leads to a diluting of the role of the sales person and limits their ability to ever reach that 'trusted advisor' status. If product

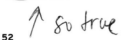
↑ so true

www.transformsales.com.au

complexity is no longer a concern for today's increasingly educated buyers, then what role does the modern day sales person play? Quote giver? Order taker? Walking brochure?

Evolution of B2B sales - power has gradually moved to the customer

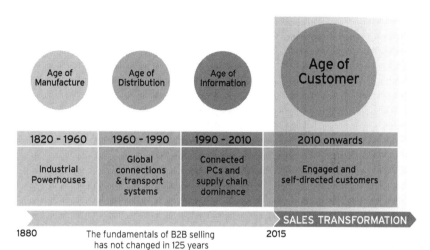

The fundamentals of B2B selling has not changed in 125 years

Adapting to this new customer-led age is going to be a challenge for many vendor sales organisations and there is a mountain of evidence and research that now supports the key tenets of this book:

- Buyers of IT products and services must do *'more business with less vendors'*.

- Vendors seem to be unaware of the importance of their place within the customers *'vendor stack'*.

- The *buying journey* no longer requires vendor input until much later in the process.

- *Cloud* is dramatically changing the way that IT products and services are acquired and consumed.

- Vendors must offer enhanced flexibility and be prepared to change their models (sharing risk with customers).

- Strategic alliance partnerships will become critical for smaller vendors.

- Vendors that fail to adapt to these changing customer requirements will be marginalized.

All things considered, the research confirms the perspective that vendor sales leaders can no longer ignore these important market trends. *Sales Transformation* is now essential for vendor sustainability.

Part Two

SALES
TRANSFORMATION

The fundamentals of B2B sales
have not changed in 130 years, and yet buyers
of technology products have dramatically changed
the way they buy. Vendors must now transform their
entire sales execution models to address
the new buying journey.

Top 10 Initiatives:

Throughout my career, one thing has remained constant in every role that I have performed and that is that every business is striving for year-on-year growth. Growth expectations always exert continuous pressure on all sales people to not only grow revenues each year but also margins and profitability. The other side of this coin for sales people is the often forgotten fact that customers always search for ways to spend less each year on the IT systems that run their businesses. In that sense, customers and vendors have always been diametrically opposed – customers endeavor to decrease annual IT spend, whilst vendors work to push more product(s) and services into the market in order to grow revenues each year.

Within this context of opposing driving forces there is a great deal of pressure on vendors to disrupt and innovate, and now more than ever before, vendors must narrow the focus of their attention onto those elements that can actually be controlled. Sales people have a tendency of deluding themselves into thinking that they can control all aspects of the sales cycle when, in my experience, this is rarely ever the case. The best thing that effective sales people can do is learn to control their actions and reactions to events that are outside their control, and to trust that the right actions will ultimately lead to positive outcomes. In the case of *Sales Transformation*, there needs to be a clear line of demarcation between the elements that we, as sales people, can control and those which we cannot. For vendor sales people in 2015, we can list some of the factors that remain outside their span of control as follows:

- External market change – Political, Economic, Socio-Cultural, Technology, Environment & Legal

- Globalization of markets – cross-border interdependence.

- Market maturation – natural market forces and industry/product lifecycles.

- Emerging technology and innovation – disruptive technological change.

- Shifting customer expectations, tastes and preferences.
- Competition – emergence of new competitors and/or substitute products.

The best sales leaders that I have come across in my career usually operate on the principle, or a variation, of *"flawless execution in everything that we control"*, and this is the basis upon which I have always tried to manage my teams. The principle is simple: Sales executives have no control over any of the factors pertaining to the external environment, so let's focus only on elements that can be controlled and ensure that we execute every aspect of the sales cycle flawlessly. On this basis, I have attempted to outline what I believe are the Top 10 Sales Transformation Initiatives for vendors in 2015, all of which are initiatives that can be controlled.

However, before we get started on my Top 10, please let me be very clear: *Sales Transformation* has many connotations and may mean different things to different people. The simplistic view that I have taken is that any change to the current sales execution model that is enacted as a result of changing buyer behaviour is, in my view, *Sales Transformation*. What we are talking about with *Sales Transformation* is a change management program that focuses largely on those customer-facing personnel within the vendor organisations, and this always requires very careful planning and execution in order to get it right. Customers now rarely give vendors a second chance if they get it wrong the first time, and whether it is a radical (*big bang*) or incremental change management approach, there is no doubt that even the smallest of changes at the sales functional level will be met with internal resistance. Like any change program, the first requirement is to have a clear view of where you are now, and where you need to be at a particular point in time, and to quickly gain senior management support for the proposed changes. Then you must create a very compelling case for change and ensure that every aspect of the transformation program is measurable and therefore manageable.

Sales Transformation, as a sustaining change program, will require each and every vendor business to conduct careful impact assessments when aligning any new initiatives with the company strategy, purpose and objectives (short, medium and long term) and, in my experience, business transformations usually don't succeed unless they deliver substantive *quick wins* within 6 to 12 months. Successful vendors build momentum by focusing first on initiatives that can make an early impact—and potentially help fund further transformation initiatives—then on building a case for further change efforts.

Throughout my career, some business leaders have taken the black and white view of categorizing business initiatives as either *tactical* or *strategic*. Depending on your definition, some of the initiatives in the next section can be classified as *tactical* and others more *strategic*, requiring more careful planning and analysis. Some organisations may find certain aspects of my Top 10 *Sales Transformation* initiatives quite simple to implement, whilst others will find even the most tactical of concepts difficult to execute. Consistently successful vendors are always thinking about what minor adjustments can be made to improve sales productivity, but it's one thing to 'strategise' about this stuff, and another thing entirely to take action. As always, company culture will be a critical success factor and, due to the distinct lack of change that has occurred in B2B sales models for the past 130+ years, I'm not suggesting that *Sales Transformation* will be easy – far from it. That said, every journey must begin with some small steps, thus, let us start by considering some ideas that I hope will provide vendor sales leaders with some food for thought on how they can transform aspects of their existing sales models to better align with the changing market conditions outlined in Part 1.

Becoming Market Sensing

Vendor sales departments spend far too much time inwardly focused. Given the rapid rate of ubiquitous change now occurring across almost every industry, it is critical that vendor sales leaders regularly 'zoom-out' and take a careful look at their respective market places and the disruptive change that is taking place in almost every area of business. It sounds so obvious, but many vendors rarely do this properly. This 'zooming out' to gather market intelligence and feeding that data back into the vendor business is one of the most overlooked aspects of the current sales person's duties. As the conduit between the organisation and its various markets, the sales person is the key link between the external environment and the business strategy that is supposed to address evolving market needs and trends. In my experience, there are very few vendor sales teams operating today that pay this important aspect of business the attention that it deserves.

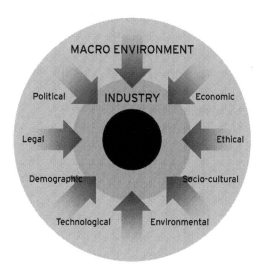

Research conducted whilst writing this book has enabled me to gather and underscore important customer insights, and there is now overwhelming evidence that vendor sales people are so heavily fixated on short term financial performance that they have completely overlooked arguably the most important element of their role – understanding the customer.

The renowned management author, G. S. Day (1994), described it best when he stated that businesses must have an *"outside-in perspective"* and become what he refers to as *"market-sensing"*. The theory being that this externally focused perspective creates a customer-centric approach that will ensure that all innovation and sales effort is actually relevant to target market requirements. There are very few vendors today that can honestly state that they are truly market sensing. On the contrary, most vendor sales departments display an "inside-out perspective" where sales people spend more time in the office than they do actually engaged with their customers and this is something that I have never understood.

As businesses grow and mature, they quite often spend so much time focused on solving the organisational problems that they gradually forget about solving customer problems. The *outside-in* approach is built on the belief that customer-centricity, emerging market needs and continuous value creation are the keys to success. Long-term shareholder value is a consequence of listening and providing value to customers and helping them to get their jobs done more effectively and efficiently than the competition, and yet almost everywhere that I look, I'm still witnessing vendor sales people neglecting this vitally important element of their role – gathering customer requirements and market intelligence.

There are two simple sets of questions that sales people should ask themselves to evaluate whether the organisation they represent leans more towards an *outside-in approach* (or the opposite *inside-out* approach):

- Do you know whom your targeted customer segments are, what needs and behaviours they have, how to best solve their relevant problems and what kind of value you provide them?

- Is there a strong fit between your target segments' needs, your value proposition, your overall business model, internal processes and a customer-oriented organisational culture, with focus on creating value for your customers? And do you feel that this is a fundamental necessity of running a successful business?

How can a business ever respond to changing market conditions if their sales people are not feeding important market intelligence back into the business? How is critical market intelligence and knowledge being managed and shared? How can a sales leader spot the next trend or growth opportunity if the vendor sales people spend most of their time internally focused? The truth is that many sales departments have been grossly underfunded when it comes to identifying trends and changes in buyer behaviour. Some vendors have become so addicted to the vast profits and revenue streams of the legacy models that they are now unable to see the waves of change that are hurtling towards them.

Vendor businesses will fail to remain relevant with their customers in these times of unprecedented change if they are not "market-sensing". Vendors that get this right are the ones that will be able spot the future pockets of growth or the next big trend. Inwardly focused vendors will remain low priority "me too" suppliers in the eyes of the customers – if they are lucky.

Sales Transformation – Next Steps:

1. Develop a heightened focus on external information gathering and knowledge management. Ensure that all sales staff become much more externally focused. Key trends and customer data must be regularly captured and shared appropriately.

2. Senior executives (C-Level) to spend one week per quarter working with the vendor sales team to ensure top-down understanding of current customer issues and market trends.

3. Investigate opportunities to utilize *Big Data* analytics to help inform market segmentation and target customer strategies.

4. Job specification amendments to include obligations for sales people to regularly feed market intelligence back into the business.

5. Remove unnecessary internal duties and refocus sales people on collecting and understanding market trend information and critical customer requirements.

Adapting to the new buying journey:

We have already established, beyond any doubt, that IT buyers no longer require the same type of relationship with their vendor sales person that they once did. Sales people have, up until now, enjoyed a model that allows them to work alongside their customers' right throughout the *buying journey* to create awareness, discover needs and then sell their solutions. Since the late 1880s, this traditional B2B sales approach has worked very well because customers didn't know how to solve their own complex problems. Those days are over – all customers are highly educated and, in my recent experience, most customers probably know more about the vendor's products than the vendor's own sales people. This problem for sales people gets even worse with younger buyers. *Gen Y* (or Millennials) customers definitely do not buy things the way that their grandparents did, so why would sales people continue to use the same approach and methodology that they have used to sell to their parents and grandparents?

Vendor involvement in the new buying journey

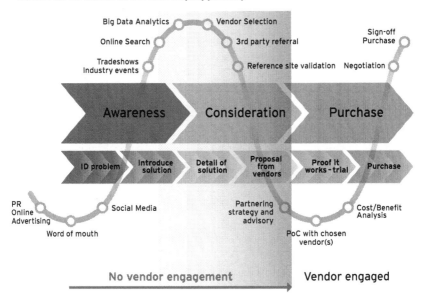

This new *buying journey* has some serious consequences for vendor sales people in that customers no longer permit the vendor salesperson to participate in the critical early stages of the sales cycle. This means that today's sales people are now less able to:

- Build trust and rapport with customer.
- Qualify and highlight customer pain.
- Gather important customer data and requirements.
- Articulate their unique value proposition.
- Differentiate from their competition.

The forced removal of some of these key elements means that the salesperson has virtually no hope of ever gaining 'trusted advisor' status. Worse still, the sales person can no longer influence customer decision-making at the various stages of the new *buying journey* and this means that the most important element of the traditional salesperson's role has now been effectively relegated to annals of history. Some industry experts are now arguing that the vendor sales role is now on a gradual transition to "walking brochure" or "quote giver". If this is even remotely accurate, then this concept alone creates some serious implications for vendor's sales people who, like me, have always been taught about the importance of being able to influence customer decision – making during the early *qualifying* stages of the sales cycle. Bluntly, if sales people are not able to participate in the qualifying stages then the concept of 'solution selling' is virtually dead.

Solution selling is dead

Brent Adamson and his colleagues at Corporate Executive Board published a ground-breaking article in Harvard Business Review (Aug, 2012) citing the *"End of Solution Sales"*. Adamson and his co-authors make the case that the best sales people are combating these new *buying journey* changes with what they termed *"insight selling"*. The publication asserts that the big challenge for sales people today is finding ways to engage the customer much earlier in the *buying journey* – ideally, even before the customer fully understands their own needs. If this is not possible, or you arrive late in the process, then the successful sales person of the future will have to become a *subject matter expert* that can swoop in and *change the game* by challenging the customer's strategy and direction with provocative insights.

This disruptive and challenging approach argued by Adamson *et al* (2012) resonates loudly with me, and will require a new breed of sales person that does actually have specialist knowledge and experience. In my view, this type of sales person is an increasingly rare animal indeed. So the key question here is: How can you turn generalist sales people into insightful, subject matter experts that have at least some degree of specialist knowledge? The answer to this question depends on how much time you have available to allow the sales person to develop this deep specialist knowledge. From my own experience, I would suggest that there is currently a very small number of IT sales people that can effectively make the transition to becoming a subject matter expert or 'insight seller' and this is largely due to the increasingly generalist and *siloed* experience of the modern sales person – not to mention the increasing transience and *job-hopping* that now plagues the increasingly commoditized IT industry.

On-boarding a new sales person and expecting them to become a subject matter expert in short order is the type of delusion that often accompanies failed sales strategies. According to a recent Accenture study, *"approximately 78% of newly-hired sales people take 6 months or more to become truly proficient at selling"*. That is, it takes at least 6 months for an IT sales person to reach the point where they can actually speak with some level of authority about their products, the industry, and their solutions. Personally, I have not seen a sales person join a new company with no prior industry experience and become a subject matter expert (the kind that customers truly value) inside 3-5 years. The cold hard reality is that, to become a subject matter expert, an IT sales person must have deep industry knowledge and vast experience about the ways in which other customers have solved problems. Personally, I believe that attempting to train every sales person to become a subject matter expert is simply a bridge too far, and that the smarter tactic rests somewhere within a team-based approach to selling – where the subject matter expert can be rolled in where and when appropriate.

The futility of cold calling

Given the above-mentioned changes, it is now practically pointless to have highly paid IT sales people spending time *cold calling*. We have already established that customers now prefer not to accept any new vendors – on the contrary, customers are actively looking to *cull* vendors wherever possible. And if you accept that customers within your industry are purposefully completing between 60-80% of the *buying journey* BEFORE they engage with vendors then a much smarter approach to prospecting for new business is now required.

What was once a vitally important component of the sales persons role in developing new business, *cold calling* now simply annoys the already overburdened IT buyers and the last thing they need is to begin a long-winded sales cycle with a new vendor. Customers now know where to go to find new technology breakthroughs – they most certainly don't need to wait for the phone to ring. People in general now despise receiving unsolicited phone calls from any person that is trying to sell something and this is certainly congruent with my own personal experience in recent times where success rates from cold calling is at the lowest levels that I have seen, and I challenge any IT vendor sales person to disagree with me on this point.

The futility of cold calling in these mature phases of the IT industry also supports my contention about the increasing movement towards team-based selling. Vendor sales people must use every tool available, including their colleagues, to identify a more intelligent path of least resistance into their target accounts – a path that raises the probability of success rather than the indiscriminate *hit and miss* (mostly miss) approach of cold calling in today's markets. Utilising social media tools (and other analytics) that might assist in gaining access to the right contacts within target accounts will be crucial for the sales people of the future. In highly competitive and mature markets success comes from who you know, not what you know, and this means that networking continues to become increasingly important. Sales leaders who insist that their sales people make *cold calls* have failed to recognize any of the important changes outlined in this book, and they will soon learn that their diminishing conversion rates from this activity will begin to severely hurt their businesses. Sales leaders that insist on making cold calling a mandatory part of the daily sales activity system are not only wasting expensive resources, they are focusing company resources in the wrong places and giving their competitors a leg up in the process. So, cease cold calling, and start to use a more intelligent form of demand creation and lead generation.

How to match the new buying journey

1 Acknowledge the new buying journey:

Given that sales people are, in most cases, arriving late into the *buying journey*, the modern sales person would now be well advised to quickly ascertain the buying preferences for each and every customer that they manage. Listed below is an example of the types of questions that a sales person must now begin to ask:

- How do you prefer the sales journey/process to unfold?
- What are the key steps in your buying cycle?
- What key outcomes do you require from a vendor's sales process?
- How can we effectively adapt our sales cycle to your buying journey?
- Can you give me an example of how one of your vendors has done a great job for you?

In my experience, today's vendor sales people rarely ask these types of important questions resulting in a distinct lack of understanding of customer expectations. Customers genuinely appreciate it when sales people do ask these sorts of questions because it not only shows that the sales person has a current understanding of the *buying journey*, but it also demonstrates to the customer that they dealing with a professional vendor organisation that understands the new age of customer experience.

2 Engage Early (where possible):

It is difficult to overstate the importance of understanding exactly what each customer wants from the sales experience, and one of the biggest challenges now facing vendors is how to get back to engaging and influencing customers upstream, early in their journey. Has the horse bolted? Or can the sales person (and his/her colleagues in marketing) find other ways to impose themselves upon the early stages of the *buying journey*? Putting marketing to one side for now (and make no mistake that awareness marketing and demand creation is now more important than ever before), sales leaders must identify creative new ways to engage buyers 'before' they are even aware that they have a problem – and I don't mean by *cold calling*. Sales leaders must ask themselves: What else can be done to help engage customers early and to create that all important mind-share? I nearly always default to leveraging *who* we know, not *what* we know and this is always a good starting point when trying to break open a new pocket of growth. Sales teams must get smarter about leveraging relationships into new opportunities to ensure that they are front and centre when a prospective customer becomes aware of a problem.

Some vendors are now spending significant funds on Executive Briefings (lunches and dinners), with some even flying existing customers to corporate headquarters and company Expos in order to demonstrate thought leadership and to help influence customer decision-making. The key objective for the vendor in this type of activity is simply to ensure customer awareness of technology roadmaps and the types of innovations that are coming so that, when the customer is finally aware of the problem (or simply looking for a new technology driven competitive advantage), the vendor is "top of mind".

3 Integrated Marketing and Big Data Analytics:

Today, almost every sale that occurs in IT involves some form of online research, consideration or purchase. The internet and *eCommerce* has created a level playing field and many organisations (not just IT vendors) are now focusing more and more resource on carefully planned and managed awareness and brand marketing in order to gain that all important *mindshare*. *Big Data* analytics and sophisticated data mining techniques are now assisting sales leaders in narrowing the focus on target customer segments (and indeed specific customer businesses) that may be just about to enter a buying cycle, and this new level of analytics will supersede the horribly outdated 'shot-gun' approach that most sales leaders still use to this day. Sadly, I know of some vendors that assign a territory to their sales people and simply send them out hunting for new customers with absolutely zero market or customer intelligence. Keeping the new *buying journey* and *vendor stack* concepts in mind, these sales leaders are unequivocally burning company resource and destroying value with this lazy and outdated approach.

Social media and social *listening* techniques can also provide businesses with critical and timely information that allows them to go beyond market research and be able to proactively target customers at the exact time that that customers become receptive. Connecting customers with one another and creating conversations and positive *buzz* is yet another way in which savvy vendors are now impacting the *buying journey* early. Social *listening* can also be used in order to quickly quash any negative sentiment/buzz (or spot competitive or political moves that may indicate risks) that is being perpetuated via the myriad of ubiquitous social media formats. Used in the right way, social media and social *listening* can also help you hear and act upon opportunities to service your customers better or to identify a key competitive advantage. Sales leaders that embrace this new era of technology and analytics will begin to develop insights that in some cases can reveal critical pockets of growth whilst simultaneously guarding against competitive threats and disruption.

The Extended Buying Journey

Everyone today is talking about customer experience (CX). Optimizing the experience that each customer has with your products and services well beyond the point of sale is a logical endeavour if you want repeat business. However, there are still far too many sales departments that do not practise what they preach in this regard, and customers can smell it a mile away. Intelligent sales people have long realize encourage customers to come back to them, they need to recognize that the way the customer experiences their product post-sale is the critical element. If you happen to be one of the vendors that does survive vendor rationalization then, whether you like it or not, you will be required to enhance every aspect of the economic value that you provide to your customers – especially after the initial sale. The new *buying journey* now extends well past the initial sale, and consumption-based models of the future will require vendors to share risk up front in return for a longer payback period. This simply spells the end of the short-term *'churn & burn'* approach that vendors have used up to this point, to be replaced by an extended and iterative sales cycle where vendors must continuously add-value post sale.

The extended buying journey of the future

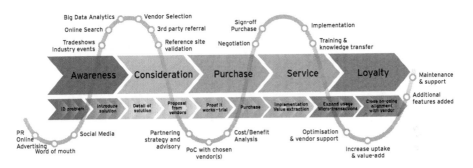

This extended buying journey really shines a light on the extent to which the current sales models are now set up to fail. With this extended commitment to adding value post sale, vendor sales people must become adept at not just selling value based on where their technology is today but also where the technology roadmap will bring new value into the future. Whilst I cringe when I hear vendor sales people talk about selling futures or vaporware, there is no doubt that customers increasingly require a long range vision from their vendors that will endure and that will be delivering value for years after the initial sale.

Sales Transformation - Next Steps:

1. More emphasis must now be placed on customer retention programs. Expanding existing customer relationships protects against being *culled* or asked to engage via a Tier 1.

2. Sales and marketing leaders must collaborate more closely to address late arrival into the new *buying journey*. Awareness and demand creation programs must be even more targeted on capturing customer attention early.

3. Investigate the use of analytics (and new technology tools like *Big Data* and social media) to apply insights to make better, more informed marketing decisions. Sales leaders must now use data-driven decision– making to better inform resource allocation and go-to-market planning.

4. Develop a fresh approach to prospecting. *Cold calling* is no longer relevant in today's mature markets.

5. Devise a training approach that can rapidly convert generalist sales people into 'subject matter experts'. Insight selling will require sales people to have deeper specialist knowledge in order to create perceived customer value.

Managing the Vendor Stack

Very few vendor sales people regularly assess where they rank on their customers "*vendor stack*" and whilst this seems like a common sense thing to do, today's sales people are so caught up in the pressure of short term revenue attainment that they either forget to ask these common sense questions, or they simply don't know that this is now an important benchmark of every customer relationship. If there is any doubt in your mind about this, then here is the test: If you are currently working as a senior executive or sales leader within a vendor business, I challenge you to ask your sales people where your company ranks on the '*vendor stack*' with each of the accounts that they manage. I'm certain that I know what response you will receive.

Within the traditional B2B sales model, the *qualifying* stages of each and every sale always requires significant amounts of time and, in some cases, large amounts of company resource. Of course, there would be little point in going through this entire *qualifying* phase, gathering and analyzing requirements, designing solutions, only to find that your customer is not permitted to accept new, or what is often referred to as 'off panel', vendors. Wouldn't it be preferable to learn that right up front? What's the point of finding out that you have just lost a customer (through being culled from the vendor stack) after the decision has already been made? Obviously, it would be preferable to identify where you stand on the vendor stack before you get culled, allowing corrective action if required. Therefore, it is my opinion that it's now much more important to understand each individual customers '*vendor stack*' than any other aspect of *qualifying* – regardless of whether or not the customer is new or existing. My point here is simply that *qualifying*, *relationship building* and searching for *pain points* is a huge waste of time and company resource until the sales person has been able to ascertain some of the fundamentals surrounding each customer's *buying journey* and their respective '*vendor stacks*'. Vendor sales people who fail to identify what is now a common customer policy for "*blocking*" new vendors will risk spending months working on what they may believe is a revenue-producing opportunity only to find that their forecasted opportunity falls over at the final hurdle. This can cripple smaller vendors and, sadly, I have seen this happen.

It almost goes without saying that engaging an end-user customer via a strategic alliance partner (Tier 1 or '*prime*' vendor) is a radically different sales model from the traditional selling direct to the end user (customer). The Tier 1 or '*prime*' vendor rightfully believes that they 'own the customer relationship' which means that a lower level (Tier 3) vendor sales person is usually required to play second fiddle. More often than not, this removes the control of the sales cycle for the second fiddler, rendering them a transactional facilitator. It means rarely getting close enough to the end user/customer to ever truly understand the requirements or the specific customer's *buying journey*, and therefore never being able to add perceived value to the end user. Under this model, sales people will rarely if ever attain trusted advisor status, and the commercial implications for the vendor extend well beyond simply relinquishing some margin to the '*prime*'.

Customer retention

Treating the customer like royalty in order to boost loyalty and advocacy should now be the main objective of every vendor business. Sadly, this is still not the case as many vendors pay lip service to being customer-centric, and this is now creating genuine risk within those customer accounts that now rank-order their vendors. Whilst upward mobility (within the 'vendor stack') is uncommon, vendors must work hard to find any means by which they can move up the 'vendor stack' in order to protect their on-going business relationship with each customer, and attempts must be made to ensure that each customer has a clear understanding of just how invaluable you are as one of their existing vendors.

As outlined earlier, my Qantas experience taught me that sitting back and assuming that your customers actually value you as their Account Manager, or your products and services, is a *fatal flaw* that is likely to cause your business (and probably your career) a significant setback.

Every sales person on the planet knows that it is always much easier to sell something new to an existing customer than it is to sell anything to a 'new' customer and yet, in the mad scramble for short term results, this important sales principle is quite often overlooked. Protecting existing customer relationships is even more critical in today's highly competitive and mature markets, and vendors will increasingly have to learn to invest in protecting their position within existing customers as a priority over the commonly sought after "net new" customer growth. The old days of what I call *"hit & run"* selling are fading into a distant memory.

It is my absolute view that any vendor that now ranks as a Tier 3 (or higher) must identify the Tier 1 *('prime')* vendors for each account and ensure that they have visibility with those vendors. That is, lower level vendors must be proactive and develop informal relationships with the Account Directors at each Tier 1 *('prime')* vendor, perhaps by offering some incentives for future sales collaboration or partnering: *"We are already a supplier, and you guys could clip our ticket on future sales in return for your support within the account"*. Converting the powerful Tier 1 *('prime')* vendor into a re-seller partner may result in a minor loss of margin in the short term, however, having a highly influential partner by your side is much better than facing the risk of being culled from the account.

To avoid any nasty surprises relating to the *'vendor stack'*, sales people must now ask the following key questions up front in the very early stages of the *qualifying* phase of the sales cycle:

NEW CUSTOMER	EXISTING CUSTOMER
Do you accept new (off-panel) vendors?	Where do we currently reside on your 'vendor stack'?
What is your process for on-boarding new vendors? Where will we rank (as a new vendor) on your 'vendor stack'?	How do you currently rank vendors? What are the key criteria against which you measure vendor performance and importance?
Are you planning to rationalize vendors in the future?	Are you planning to rationalize vendors in the future?

Great question

more...

NEW CUSTOMER	EXISTING CUSTOMER
Who are the key people in your organisation that new vendors should get to know?	How can we move up your 'vendor stack'? Where can we add more value to your business?
What key metrics do you use in measuring new vendor performance?	Are there any Tier 1 ('prime') vendors that you think we should be engaged with?

Vendors that adopt these strategies can potentially insulate themselves within important accounts, and ensuring that sales people ask these important questions (above) must now become a standard part of every vendor's retention strategies.

Becoming integral to the customer's technology ecosystem

Another recent sales experience that provided my team with some valuable learning was the recent case where we were being gradually marginalized by a large existing customer here in Australia. At the time, we were a Tier 3 supplier on this particular customer's *vendor stack* and we began to see the signs that we were at risk within this account. As is now common practice, this customer was engaging in some good old-fashioned 'vendor bashing' – which, for the uninitiated, is the concept whereby customers find (and in some cases fabricate) any reason that they can to complain about a perceived lack of value being received from you as the vendor. Customers will often engage in this tired old game of brinkmanship in the hope that they will gain a price reduction or *better deal* from the vendor, and we had become used to this treatment from this particular customer. Unfortunately for many vendors, inexperienced sales leaders who are already under pressure are usually very quick to oblige the vendor-bashing customer, especially when they are a large and important client. Succumbing to this pressure often costs vendors large slices of margin.

As mentioned, this particular customer was well known in the Australian IT industry for 'vendor bashing', and they were threatening (we assumed bluffing) to *"rip & replace"* our technology with a substitute product from an existing Tier 1 supplier. This meant that my team was now faced with the challenge of rapidly assessing the extent to which our product was being utilized, where it was adding value, along with how integral our technology is within the customer's operating architecture and end-user environments. The end game here was to assess the impact that would be incurred by our customer if they did actually make good on their threat to boot us to the curb. Having identified how and where our product was being used, we became aware that our technology was in fact integral to technology platform, meaning that a *rip & replace* was going to be high risk and costly for our customer. The footnote to this story is that our customer knew all of that, which confirmed that they were in fact bluffing. We stood firm on our quote, and the relationship continued. Herein lies the issue with this shifting power base – customers can now demand more from each and every vendor, and this is the new reality that sales people must address.

Sales Transformation - Next Steps:

In order to avoid being culled or asked to engage via a Tier 1 (*'prime'*), vendors must embrace the following:

1. Identify where you currently reside on the *'vendor stack'* with each and every existing customer. If it's a new customer that you have never sold to before, then it's critical to establish whether or not the new customer will actually accept new (*'off-panel'*) vendors?

2. Distinguish any means by which you can move up the *'vendor stack'*.

3. Highlight any areas of the customer technology eco-system where your product is *integral* to your customer's business operations. Leverage this position and ensure that the customer's vendor management and procurement personnel are aware of

your *integral* position and the value-add that you bring to their business. Work hard to ensure end-user productivity.

4. Clarify the overall vendor landscape with each account. Focus on ascertaining who the Tier 1 ('prime') vendors are within the customer's *'vendor stack'*. Identify any personal connections with Tier 1 *('prime')* vendors that may be able to be leveraged.

5. Commence informal relationship development with existing Tier 1 *('prime')* vendors for each key account as part of a defensive (retention) strategy. If the Tier 1 ('prime') vendors don't know you, they can't help you.

Sales Qualifying and the Forecast

Since the earliest incarnations of the current B2B sales model (dating back to the 1880s), sales people have been trained constantly on the importance of *qualifying* the prospective customer to ensure complete and full understanding of the customer needs or *pain points*, and yet we have already established that most of these generally accepted practices around sales qualifying are now increasingly out of step with the modern *buying journey*. As previously discussed, sales people are rarely getting a chance to use their *qualifying* skills and techniques due to the fact that customers no longer permit the vendor sales person to take part in these early stages of the *buying journey*. Putting qualifying to one side for now, it's important to understand some of this historical context as we begin to identify areas where transformation will challenge some long-held beliefs around sales.

A "Numbers Game"

Let me quickly dispel an important myth. In my very first sales role (back in 1989,) I was taught that sales was simply a *numbers game*: *"Make 100 cold calls, and you will likely yield approximately 30 interested parties, of which you should obtain 10 appointments, ultimately leading to 3 closed sales."*

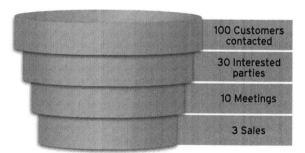

100 Customers contacted

30 Interested parties

10 Meetings

3 Sales

3% conversion rate
from cold calling

To this day, many industries still believe in a version of the 'numbers game', but I can assure you that sales in the customer-led age is most definitely **not** a numbers game. Even as a rookie sales guy, I instinctively knew that the numbers game concept had some fatal flaws. Nevertheless, the concept made some sense from the point of view that every successful sales person MUST constantly prospect for new buyers to build and continuously refill the sales pipeline in order to create a consistent flow of sales conversions. This is 'pipeline management 101', and yet I'm astonished to find sales leaders that still use this type of 'numbers game' logic and associated micro-management techniques in today's modern context. Why hire professional and highly-paid sales people if you are going to treat them like robots? If your sales leaders are still managing by this outdated thinking then it might be time to review the leadership that is running, or should I say *ruining*, your business.

Customer converstion ratio

When you boil it down, sales people are actually assessed on their ability to convert a *prospect* into a paying *customer*, and most businesses use varying methods for measuring conversion rates. Some sales people seem to be instinctively good at "closing" and some just never seem to be able to take a prospect through from awareness to close. Whilst sales leaders have always grappled with conversion rates, I have always found that it comes down to some important basics: If the sales person has *qualified* correctly and managed each stage of the sales cycle appropriately, then *'conversion'* becomes a logical conclusion – all things being equal. The secret here is getting the *qualifying* right, and this is now more important than ever before against the backdrop of the new *buying journey*.

Sales leadership, coaching and mentoring are now critical to ensure that sales people are performing each step in the sales cycle adequately. The good old days when the sales leader sat in the office (as a 'sales spectator') are over. Sales leaders must now roll-up their sleeves and participate by coaching and mentoring their sales teams to improve all aspects of sales execution. If your company currently has a 'sales spectator' leading the sales department from the comfort of his/her office, then you would be better placed hiring a graduate accountant to be the sales leader – not only will it be more cost effective, but the graduate accountant will also be much better than the 'sales spectator' at playing the 'numbers games'. Sadly, both will fail in this new customer age.

By the way, I'm not suggesting that sales leadership is the only answer to improving conversion ratios. There will always be a percentage of sales that fall through the cracks but, assuming there is a genuine buyer and a properly-executed sales cycle, then conversion rates should become far more predictable.

In my most recent role, my team and I implemented a very simple system that rapidly translated to an important increase in our conversion rate. To achieve this, we conducted some detailed analysis into our historical sales data, and we questioned some of the long-held beliefs and metrics around pipeline management and conversion rates. Through some careful analysis, we quickly learned that, out of every 10 live opportunities that had progressed to "proposal stage" (60% completion), we were converting, on average, 3 of these 10 into closed sales resulting in revenue for the company. That is, 30% conversion or *win* rate from "proposal stage" which is actually high, but then we were the market leader in our space at that time. In search of an uplift in conversion, we then decided to trial a new approach that would mean each sales person would have to become even more uncompromising and almost brutal about the way that they were qualifying opportunities which in some cases meant *qualifying out* (strategically withdrawing) from any sales opportunities where we believed that we were being used as *'column fodder'* (see section on page 83). *Qualifying out* of an opportunity is a very difficult thing for most sales people to do because sales people are, by their very nature, highly optimistic animals (wishful thinkers in fact)… always believing that they can win the deal. Sales people who manage their territories through the lens of the proverbial rose-coloured glasses are a real danger to most businesses –and I'll come back to this later.

We began approaching *qualifying* from the opposite direction – by providing small incentives (or rewards/spiffs) to sales people to *qualify out* of an opportunity rather than clinging desperately to a 'stuck' sale that in reality was never going to close. This pipeline cleansing can be scary for most sales leaders because we are all taught that you must have at least 2-5 times your quota in your pipeline to be successful, and this is really yet another anachronism that, in my opinion, has no place in modern sales planning. Allow let me explain why: As mentioned earlier, my team and I had a conversion rate of circa 30% meaning that, out of every 10 opportunities that had progressed through to Sales Stage 5 (Proposal) in our Forecast, we were converting only 3. By implementing some increased rigour around 'qualifying out' we were able to change some entrenched behaviours and reduce the 10 opportunities in Proposal Stage down to 7 whilst still converting 3 as closed sales. In other words, we began focusing on 'qualifying out' of any opportunities that were 'stuck deals' or where we were being used as 'column fodder'. The principle here was that, instead of closing 3 out of 10 opportunities, we were now in effect closing 3 out of 7. This results in an instant increase from 30% to 42% in conversion rate, not to mention the HUGE *opportunity cost* that we had just removed through 'qualifying out' of any opportunities where we didn't have:

- Strong technical fit and some perceived (by the customer) competitive advantage.

- Senior level relationship(s) with the key decision-maker or influencer.

This uplift in conversion rate, and clearer focus on *qualifying*, created a significant productivity improvement which flowed through to impact our bottom-line, and the truth is that this was a simple and easy to implement transformation that provided our business with a quick win. This is clear proof that simply focussing on building a large pipeline (2 – 5 times quota) is the wrong approach. To be clear, I'm not suggesting that pipeline development is not important, but in this modern age of selling, it's critical to ensure quality rather than quantity when it comes to the pipeline of opportunities.

I firmly believe that sales people must now become uncompromising and almost ruthless about how they qualify sales opportunities. Greater emphasis must now be placed on carefully selecting which opportunities to pursue whilst also being prepared to 'qualify out' of opportunities where you arrive late into the buying journey. If there is no pre-existing relationship and no understanding of the 'vendor stack' or the customer's new vendor policies, then the sales person now runs the risk of wasting huge amounts of company time and resource chasing a deal that they will never win. Salespeople must absolutely learn to embrace the strategic withdrawal and walk away – without ever burning the bridge, of course. The ancillary benefit in gracefully withdrawing is that customers will respect you more for being an astute business professional, and I have personally been involved in many cases where a customer has come back (cap in hand) to the vendor who politely withdrew their bid. Try it with those stuck deals, and redirect your resources onto deals that can actually be converted.

Trusted advisor status

If solution selling is, in fact, dead (as outlined in the previous section), then it is my contention that the idea of gaining 'trusted advisor' status with customers is now also dying a gradual death. In the past, successful sales people were normally viewed as a 'trusted advisor' due to their unique knowledge about the industry, their product(s) and the associated features, advantages and benefits. However nowadays, sales people have little chance of ever attaining the highly sought-after status of 'trusted advisor', in part because of the changed buying journey, but mostly because the customer is now just as knowledgeable as the IT sales person. In fact, I would argue that most customers now have a broader base of IT knowledge than most of today's IT sales people with their narrow or siloed experience and skillsets.

With new levels of knowledge, along with their access to information sources, customers can no longer afford the time to meet with a sales person that doesn't appear to have any valuable knowledge to impart. As outlined in my Qantas example, customers are dealing with vast numbers of sales people from the hundreds, if not thousands, of vendors in their vendor stack – not to mention all the new vendors that are constantly knocking on their door. If vendor sales people are NOT producing value, beyond simply providing a quote, or fulfillment/ transaction services then customers can't afford to engage with them.

Vendors must rapidly:

- Define criteria that constitutes a *trusted advisor* within a specific business or industry context.

- Ascertain which sales individuals 'could' actually reach the status of *trusted advisor* or "insight seller".

- Allow answers to the two points above to inform a revised team-based approach to selling where specialist sales resources *(trusted advisors)* can be utilized across functions, territories and *lines of business.*

Critical

What is the point of having a highly experienced, knowledgeable and credible resource that is able to gain *trusted advisor* status, confined to one particular territory or set of accounts? Wouldn't it be sensible to maximize those strengths wherever possible by establishing a new approach to collaborative or team-based sales force execution? The obvious answer is yes, and yet making these sorts of changes is almost always met with resistance because vendor sales leaders can't afford to miss any short term performance goals.

Size of pipeline

As discussed in previous section, IT sales people are normally required to provide a forward-looking sales pipeline that is some sort of multiple of the quota. In most cases, this figure is at least 2–5 times quota as a general guide to ensuring there is enough potential business in the pipeline to guarantee quota attainment. These arbitrary and often outdated *rules of thumb* usually create the wrong behaviours, and this one in particular drives sales people to manufacture (in some cases fabricate) invalid revenue opportunities that simply moves from month to month and ends up in the system as 'stuck deals'. If vendors ever bothered to look seriously at the real cost of having numerous sales people focused solely on the quantity of deals in pipeline, rather than the quality of those opportunities, they would never allow this absurd practice to continue. Sadly, this is exactly what most second-rate sales leaders do – they emphasize the importance of developing big pipelines (minimum 2–3 times quota, but essentially the bigger the better) and then they wonder why the sales person never seems to convert.

With the erroneous focus on pipeline quantity, it usually follows that, about 12–18 months later, the sales leader works out that the sales person is manipulating the pipeline and not closing any deals. By this time, the damage to the territory, and I would argue, the company brand and reputation, is already done. Many years ago, I stopped putting pressure on my sales people to manufacture a large pipeline, and instead, I refocused them on ensuring the quality of the deals in the pipeline. I even provided rewards and incentives for *qualifying out* of deals that had low probability and we would then remove them from the pipeline. Result: Forecast accuracy improved dramatically, and I always had a clearer business snapshot (month to month) to report to my senior management colleagues who were then able to plan the business activities with a much higher degree of certainty around my forecasted revenues.

Column Fodder

With many buyers now aiming to reduce the number of vendors with whom they engage, the sales people of the future will be required to become much more strategic and selective about where, and in what quantity, they commit company resource to pursuing new business opportunities. Being called into a sales opportunity late nearly always suggests that the vendor is simply being used as 'column fodder'.

Let me explain: In the normal course of procuring most 'big ticket' items, businesses usually put in place policies requiring their managers to obtain bids from more than one vendor (typically three or more). In most cases, by the time the *buying journey* reaches the *Consideration* stage, the decision is already geared towards the incumbent, or a preferred vendor, and the other two vendors are simply making up the numbers (see 'column fodder' on next page). Whilst this 'column fodder' principle is not new, it is much more relevant today than ever before, courtesy of the changes in the *buying journey*.

In the previous pages, I said that sales people who view their opportunities through rose-coloured glasses are now a real danger to vendor businesses. To be clear, if vendor sales leaders took the time to calculate the vast amount of company resource that is invested in *qualifying* and preparing responses to customer proposals (or bids), including the 'opportunity cost' of being focused on the wrong deals, they would never allow wishful thinking sales people to allocate scarce company resource without some serious scrutiny. If any other business department gambled company resource so recklessly, there would be consequences, and yet unwitting vendor sales people can cost their companies significant sums of money when they fail to properly qualify these *'column fodder'* scenarios.

The good news is that this is not a difficult transformation to make. All it takes is to ensure that sales people are coached on how to become brutal when *qualifying* by asking some difficult questions and learning how to conduct some cold hard and honest analysis to reach the right conclusions. Vendor sales people must become absolutely uncompromising in how they qualify in and out of each and every sales opportunity because the 'column fodder' principle is now a critical risk that vendors must mitigate.

The Column Fodder Principle

Under increasing competitive pressure, sales people will nearly always seek to find the path of least resistance and, whilst understandable, it can no longer be accepted that sales people simply *load up* the pipeline with all manner of opportunities in order to make it appear as though they are being "productive". This practice (by salespeople) is an ever-present danger to business and I have personally witnessed vendor businesses descend into a death spiral due to poor or erroneous pipeline management – in particular, smaller vendors where the predictability of cash-flows are critical.

Another common practice of second rate sales leaders is the folly of allowing large amounts of sales operations and resources to be consumed by a small percentage of the opportunities. Pareto's much loved '80/20' rule is applicable in so much of the modern sales forecasting approach, but allowing 80% of your sales resource to focus on 20% of your opportunities (or customers) nearly always leads to 'lumpy' forecasts – lose a couple of important deals and the pipeline is decimated. In this new era, sales leaders must become much more discerning about how and where important sales resources are allocated. It continues to provide me with a source of bewilderment that many businesses today are extremely careful about resource allocation (in order to optimize return on assets) in almost every business function and department – except sales.

Sales Transformation - Next Steps:

1. Review current approach to *qualifying* and the related forecasting practices.

2. Devise some new sales policy guidelines – carefully selecting which opportunities to pursue. Reward sales people for *'qualifying out'* of opportunities where you arrive late into the *buying journey*.

3. Being used as *column fodder* will become the norm and sales people must be trained to identify when this is happening. If there is no pre-existing relationship, no understanding of the *'vendor stack'* or the customer's new vendor policy then sales people must strategically withdraw or risk wasting valuable company resource.

4. Identify 'stuck deals' and qualify out where appropriate, ensuring that the withdrawal is executed politely and gracefully. Customers often come back when you walk away.

5. Review sales training practices and identify which sales individuals could be trained to reach *trusted advisor* levels – and which ones can't.

6. Engage an experienced Sales Coach to ensure all sales people understand the dangers associated with the new *buying journey* and the *column fodder* principle.

Focus on Financial Metrics:

Sales people are constantly reminded about the importance of accurate forecasting, and yet my experience tells me that the majority of today's sales people have heard their manager harping on about forecasting so often that its importance has been gradually diminished over time. In my experience, there is little to be gained by simply barking orders at the sale people about how *"forecasting is important"* if you don't explain why and then give them the tools by which to ensure this accuracy. Sales people should be educated about some of the specific business fundamentals and key financial metrics that drive business planning, performance and sustainability. Some of these fundamentals are as follows:

- Cost of Sales
- Cost Per Employee
- Revenue Per Employee
- Contribution Margin (per product/unit)
- Expense to Revenue Ratio
- Profit Per Employee
- Average Order Value
- Average Cost Per Sale
- Sales Cycle Time
- Cost-Volume Ratios, and Break-Even Analysis
- EBIT

These are just some of the key financial and accounting measurements that I truly believe should be shared with the sales department in this modern era of business, and yet every business that I have worked in prefers to 'shield' the sales team from these important business metrics in order to allow them to simply focus on selling. This is narrow and outdated thinking, and I can prove it.

Latest management theory suggests that, as an effective leader, it is your responsibility to ensure that the *direction, purpose, vision* and *objectives* of your business are clearly understood and, to do this successfully, you must provide at least some degree of rationale to support these objectives if you are ever going to achieve 'willing cooperation' from your followers. Truly effective leaders rarely stand up and proclaim that *"we are headed in this direction so start paddling".* This old-school *'command and control'* model rarely results in *'willing cooperation'* and that is why it is rarely used in these modern times except in some military contexts. I have seen quite a few sales leaders lose their team's *hearts and minds* through this type of hubris. How can you expect sales people (wishful thinking optimists) to become uncompromising and brutal about how they 'qualify out' of opportunities if you don't also explain the underlying financial reasons why this is now so vitally important? Why should sales people care about inaccurate forecasting if they don't understand the serious knock-on effects that are usually caused in business planning and operations?

As an experiment a few years ago, I began sharing some of these key financial metrics (with a focus on the cost side) with my teams in order to help the sales people better understand concepts that can have a big impact on profitability – in this particular case, *Expense to Revenue* ratio was our key business metric. One area of focus was cost of sales and this helped to highlight what an hour of each sales person's time was actually costing our business. Most of my team had never previously been exposed to this type of financial accounting data and sharing it proved to be a master stroke, if I do say so myself. Not only did the team have a new appreciation and focus on measuring and managing our costs, but they also gained an understanding of *activity-based costing, cost of sales* and *contribution margin.* All of these measurements also help to bring into focus the downside of 'opportunity costs' associated with allocating company resource to the wrong (*column fodder*) opportunities. Of course, focusing resource on the wrong sales opportunities is the quickest way to grow the business of your competitors.

In my opinion, two of the best known and most effective means by which to refocus the sales teams is around Average Order Value (AOV), and Average Sales Cycle Time (ASCT). All things being equal, and in the absence of any increase in sales resources, these two important metrics are two of the best levers that sales management can utilize to generate an uplift in sales productivity. The assumption is that you can only physically manage and process a certain number of transactions each period (or quarter/month) with a set amount of sales resources available. It nearly always varies according to the individual, but each sales person can only manage a certain number of sales opportunities at any given point in time. Gaining an understanding of the maximum production efficiency for each individual member of the sales team allows the sales leader to begin to conduct what I believe is vitally important business analysis into *total sales capacity*. If you agree with me on this, then it follows that it is really only possible to increase total sales output by one of two means:

1. Increase the AOV to produce greater revenue for the same number of transactions.

2. Compress the ASCT to facilitate more transactions within the same time period.

I'm routinely surprised at how often vendor sales leaders fail to employ these two fundamental business concepts. Let us briefly focus on each one individually:

Average Order Value (AOV)

Increasing AOV is a simple, but often disregarded, method by which sales leaders can attain an uplift in sales performance, and it really is as simple as creating some increased focus on each and every transaction. Whilst the terms *cross-selling* and *up-selling* are drastically overused these days, the concepts remain valid in practically every selling context and in every market globally. IT buyers are nearly always happy to receive some sort of discounted additional extra for their purchase, and vendors should be delighted with every extra dollar of revenue that can be recognized per transaction. I always think of the 16-year-old McDonalds employee who is trained to always ask *"Would you like some fries with that?"*. Strangely, I know lots of professional IT sales people, who earn many orders of magnitude more than the average McDonalds worker, that simply forget to ask their customers any of the basic *up-sell* questions. Why?

Looking a little deeper, some of this comes back to the tyranny of short-termism which creates huge pressure for the IT sales person to URGENTLY close the sale. Some sales people either forget to ask the *up-sell* questions whilst others are so worried about the possibility of complicating the deal that they deliberately avoid going down that path with their customers. One example that springs to mind was the time, not so long ago, that one of my sales people was awaiting one final purchase order from a customer to take her over her annual quota. The deal was approved and awaiting final sign-off when she thoughtfully suggested to her customer (the decision-maker) that they really should consider attaching some professional services to the product purchase simply to be used for training and implementation services on an *as-needs* basis. Knowing that the customer had some left over budget available, she offered the customer an attractive bundled discount as an incentive, and the customer agreed. This was a simple *win-win* that added a further AUD $9,000 to the deal – a great example of up-selling to increase AOV. Sadly for this savvy sales person, the customer was forced to go back through the approval process which delayed the entire purchase order by 3 weeks resulting in this sales person missing her annual quota and the bonuses and Annual Club Trip that went along with total quota achievement. In this particular case, the sales person was adversely impacted by increasing the order value simply due to a timing issue, but she did the right thing by the company, and the customer, and unintentionally got a head-start on quota achievement for the following year.

Whether by *carrot* or *stick*, every IT sales leader ought to be able to create some much needed focus on increasing the AOV such that, in every instance where it is possible (putting aside situations where budget is completely locked down), the sales person should attempt to leverage all available options to increase the total sale value. Whilst "tying", "bundled discounting" and "rebates" are often looked upon as passé in this modern era of selling, some of these old strategies can still achieve a quick win for both customer and vendor.

By constantly reminding my sales team about the importance of increasing sales value, we managed to take our AOV from AUD $79,400 up to AUD $90,520k within a single 12 month period – a 14% revenue uplift which was achieved simply by creating some focus on financial metrics like AOV. Another unbelievably simple method for increasing AOV is to just increase your prices. Don't laugh – I'm astounded at how many vendors are too frightened to inform their customers that their prices have gone up...just like everyone else's. I have witnessed many sales people fall for that old customer trick of saying "We only have budget for x amount", resulting in the sales person defaulting straight to the lowest discount allowable. Gullible sales people that are tasked with annual renewals also often fall for that old chestnut of "We've only budgeted for the amount we paid last year". Rubbish – customers (certainly the financial and procurement personnel) build increases into their budgeting each year, and they fully expect IT prices to go up. Savvy vendors can cherry pick certain products for a price increase and, if they carefully manage their customer expectations by providing ample prior warning, their customers nearly always accept that vendors have to increase prices each year. Again, I'm astounded at how many sales leaders take the path of least resistance when it comes to placing a value on their products. Sales 101 says that if you have qualified properly, and measured the financial cost of the customer's problem, then price becomes a non-issue anyway. Raise your prices and see what happens.

Average Sales Cycle Time (ASCT)

Sales leaders who actually have their finger on the pulse will know intimately the steps involved in the typical sales cycle for each and every product (and service) that they push into their target markets. Moreover, these savvy sales leaders will always be searching for ways in which to compress the time (and therefore cost) that it takes to bring each sales opportunity to close. ASCT has always been a fundamental sales metric and a simple way for sales leaders to gain a broad understanding of total sales capacity for each team or department, which should then inform the entire go-to-market planning process – from coverage model to quota setting.

B2B sales people are usually experienced in multiple-opportunity management. That is, they must have the ability to manage multiple accounts and sales opportunities simultaneously. When it comes to coverage models, one of the fundamental questions that vendors must ask themselves is: "Can we adequately manage and facilitate all the sales opportunities that exist within a given market segment given a set number of resources?" I never cease to be amazed at how many businesses have no idea of how many actual sales opportunities their team can adequately manage and process at any given point in time. Coverage model planning is pointless without these metrics.

Yes, some sales people are better than others at juggling multiple opportunities at the one time, and yes, it is nearly always the customer's *compelling event* that dictates the sales cycle time. However, like AOV, if the sales people are not constantly looking for ways to improve the ASCT, then naturally they won't find them. Simple as that.

ASCT has always provided my businesses with a strong guide as to how many sales are actually possible within a given period, and I have always used this important data for strategic business planning. ASCT can then simply be extrapolated out over the total number of sales resources available to provide a good indicator of the total possible revenue for a period (for a set number of resources) if the sales execution plan is fully optimized.

Sales Cycle Time

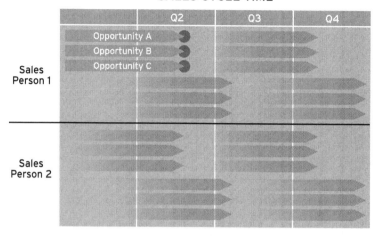

SALES CYCLE TIME

If we accept that there is indeed an ASCT, then it stands to reason that, if the average can be compressed, then we could process more transactions within the same period. Thus, the focus on reducing sales cycle time is actually all about allowing sales people to manage more sales (through to conclusion) within the same time-frame. From my own experience, this is yet another simple but often overlooked lever that sales leaders can use in the search for a quick win or productivity gain, and this should translate to some sort of uplift in sales revenue.

Put simply, ASCT x AOV equals total revenue capacity, and this should be the starting point for all sales planning, including providing an *evidence-based* guide for quota setting. Highlighting ASCT and or AOV as key measurements or KPI's will result in the sales team consciously looking for ways to make those incremental improvements so that, when added up over the period of a year, this can make a significant difference to revenue attainment. As the old saying goes, in order to manage something, you first must be able to measure it, and my experience tells me that bringing these key measurements into focus will pay dividends.

Conversely, if the sales leader never mentions these types of financial performance metrics, then the sales people will simply revert to doing what they have always done. To that end, *Sales Transformation* (at a more tactical level) is sometimes as simple as refocusing the attention of the sales personnel on the things that actually produce the results. And yet so many sales leaders fail to recognize this rudimentary aspect of performance management.

Sales Transformation - Next Steps:

1. Begin involving sales personnel in the key financial measurements that run your business. Excluding sales people from important financial metrics is divisive and counterproductive.

2. Create focus on metrics that can drive sales performance uplift – AOV and ASCT are two examples.

3. Formally notify your customers about an impending price increase – they will be expecting it.

Shifting Business Models:

Being forced to offer new and more flexible commercial models is rarely greeted with enthusiasm by vendors. Short term performance pressures dictate that vendors are always reluctant to move away from their established (and often very lucrative) business models to allow greater flexibility for their customers. The mere suggestion to IT vendors that a change in business, licensing or pricing models might be a good idea is normally met with a sharp intake of breath, followed by: *"Don't be ridiculous, we have always sold our products this way"*. I can attest to this fact, because I have personally attempted to suggest to my US-based senior management counterparts *"Times are changing and perhaps we need to be more flexible"*. I was shut down faster than an atheist at a Hill Song Convention.

Whether they like it or not, vendors must now begin to take action and become more flexible with their business models, and many are already taking the first tentative steps down this path. It is clear that customers are now migrating increasingly large proportions of their annual IT spend over to flexible *consumption-based* models and managed service offerings. IDC is forecasting 23.5% CAGR in *cloud*-based delivery of IT products, against the correspondingly small 3.1% CAGR for the industry overall. Those vendors that are not re-engineering their products into 'service-based' product bundles suitable for *cloud* delivery are not just missing this enormous growth opportunity, but they also at risk of being marginalized by their customers.

In November, 2011, Wood, Hewlin & Lah co-authored a wonderfully insightful book entitled *Consumption Economics: The New Rules of Tech*. This publication speaks directly to my point about the impending death of legacy vendor models in these modern times of *cloud* computing and the new customer-led economy. Winners and losers in this space will be shaped by the organisational decisions made by vendors in the next 2-4 years. As pointed out by Wood et al (2011), vendors must soon make the hard decisions to move away from the short term financial performance focus that drives their share price and the associated self-interests of senior management executives. Quite rightly, customers now demand a "risk shift" and the expectation is that vendors must become increasingly more flexible in the way that they license and sell their products in the future. Some savvy vendors are now also creating "customer equity" programs – giving back to customers through risk sharing and flexible loyalty programs. However, those vendors that fail to enact some of these expected changes to their business, licensing and pricing models will be marginalized by their customers in favor of those vendors that are prepared to change.

History now demonstrates that vast numbers of established IT vendors have made super profits and built vast corporations through the legacy business models of the past, and it is little wonder that there is a reluctance by many of these same vendors to change focus and move away from these lucrative models. Not only are these legacy models highly profitable for vendors, but their share price is driven by their constant growth expectations. The tyranny of short-termism is alive and well in the world of high tech with a continuing focus on short term (monthly and quarterly) results driving almost every aspect of business operations. However, the real issue here is the old chestnut of being able to balance short-term profit maximization with the long-term sustainability.

Good luck to that newly-appointed CEO of a high-tech vendor who stands up at his first AGM and states *"We are moving away from the old models to embrace a more sustainable long-term approach that will ensure higher levels of customer satisfaction…oh, and by the way, this will mean some dramatic reductions in growth and profit for us over the next few years"*. This CEO is likely to face a massive backlash from certain company stakeholder groups – especially equity-owning stakeholders.

Selling IT products and services through a Tier 1 (*'prime'*) partner is going to become the new normal for many vendors as enterprise customers insist on altering their engagement models for smaller vendors. Australian IT veteran and serial entrepreneur, Alan (Kingy) King, spotted this trend years ago and set up a business (called A2Zoutcomes) to address this important market need. Alan recently told me "*Vendors can be likened to fruit growers – vendor A sells Apples, vendor B sells Oranges, vendor C sells Bananas. However, what the customer really wants is a Fruit Salad*". A2Zoutcomes helps facilitate these much-needed engagement models by bringing vendors together, along with finance options, to provide a single aggregated interface to the customer. Today's IT buyers quite rightly expect a coordinated and intelligent engagement from their vendors, and they absolutely demand that vendor sales people have done their homework before engaging.

As previously outlined, the difficult part here for vendors is that even the smallest changes to vendor business models can sometimes mean a radical change in how revenue is generated and recognized, and this often presents vendor management with significant challenges in convincing equity-owning stakeholders that reduced earnings and profit growth in the short-term will lead to greater sustainability in the medium to longer term.

Sales Transformation – Next Steps:

1. Conduct a survey of existing customers to gauge appetite for new business models. Feedback may surprise.

2. Challenge the *status-quo* with small incremental changes to existing business models that focus on improving customer outcomes.

3. Ensure customer understanding of your business rationale for any changed models – when customers see that their vendors are attempting to *do the right thing* by them, they are less likely to relegate you (or cull) to the bottom of the vendor stack.

4. Vendor senior management must now begin to take steps towards becoming more flexible with their business models. Offering new *consumption-based* models will be crucial to vendor survival.

Team-Based Selling

The new era of sales collaboration

The role of the professional IT salesperson (Account Manager, Business Development Manager, etc) has always been a multifaceted role requiring a diverse range of skills. In this rapidly changing high tech industry, it is difficult to comprehend why so little has changed in the way that vendor sales people operate. In 27 years of selling, I have not seen a single sales leader that has ever attempted to truly challenge the traditional approach to B2B sales. Of course, this is not surprising given that vendors have been basking in the glory of massive year-on-year growth – *"if it ain't broke, don't fix it"*. No surprise that the fundamental approach used today by sales teams around the world is primarily the same approach that I first learned back in the early 1990s.

Justin Roff-Marsh, an international business consultant and the founder of Sales Process Engineering (SPE), published an interesting book in 2011 entitled *The Machine*. The book identifies some ideas on how future sales teams will collaborate while allocating certain skills and competencies where they can be most valuable. In particular this book highlights that the *division of labour* is applied to every business function (manufacturing, finance, marketing, etc.) except, strangely, to sales. The same tired and outdated B2B sales models are still being used in sales departments, and there is no doubt that all vendors must now embrace performance management strategies that enable each sales person to optimize their individual strengths, whilst also avoiding activity that exposes their weaknesses. To that end, what's the point of allowing your worst presenter to deliver a critical presentation to an important client simply because it is his or her territory? I have seen many IT sales organisations take that risk and it nearly always costs the vendor, whilst simultaneously assisting your competitors – ridiculous when you think about it.

In my last role, my team and I decided upon some simple parameters in this regard – we agreed that any sales opportunities above a certain revenue level would invoke some subtle changes in team composition and resource allocation at certain key points in the sales process. This was done simply to maximize our strengths through more intelligent coordination of resources whilst at the same time limiting areas of weakness. Intuitively, this concept makes sense, however, nothing is ever as simple as it first appears when it comes to business transformations in general. This type of restructuring is difficult primarily because of the challenges that it creates with team composition, performance assessments and sales force compensation among other things.

Team composition

Nearly every sales team that I have worked in has contained a mixture of sales types and, whilst there are many differing views on how to categorize sales people, the following best reflects my own experience in high technology B2B vendor sales:

1. **The Hunter.** The hunter (often referred to as the 'lone wolf') is after the big kill and will work for a long time to get a deal finalized. However, the hunter may not be the best choice for establishing long-term client relationships.

2. **The Farmer.** The farmer is skilled at cultivating long-term relationships with his or her clients. If you want a very close and personal engagement with your customers, the farmer is right for your business.

3. **The Scout.** When expanding into a new market in your industry, it's tempting to move your top sales person to the new geographical territory. But since the person is unfamiliar with the area, it's better to hire a scout who hails from that market, preferably from one of your major competitors.

4. **The Shepherd.** If you are expanding and offering new product lines, you need a shepherd, someone who is a widely recognized industry expert. This person will bring in a whole flock of followers.

In my experience, the 'Hunters' are increasingly rare and this not a bad thing given that the old *'churn & burn'* models of the past that suited 'Hunters' are almost extinct. Buyer behaviour now requires vendor sales people to become closer, for longer, with their customers meaning that 'Farmers' will become the dominant sales type. Regardless of which method is used to broadly pigeon-hole your sales people, one thing is universally true – all sales people have their strengths and weaknesses, and great sales teams comprise a mixture of these sales types.

Those of us that have been in sales for any length of time know that some sales people are great at developing *trust and rapport* with customers, and some are better at the transactional back-office components. Some are excellent presenters, and some should never stand up in front of a prospective customer audience. And yet, I know lots of vendors that are still relying on the same old outdated sales models that positions the sales person effectively as an *'autonomous agent'* to whom they say: *"Here is your list of accounts (territory), there's the phone, start selling"*. Those days are well and truly over. The savvy sales leaders of today (and tomorrow) now also understand that age-diversity across the sales team can have its advantages. Gen-Y or Millennial sales people are much more likely to embrace concepts such as the use of social media and predictive analytics than some of the old school sales types that have entrenched behaviours that are often difficult to change.

Team-based selling

Further to the previous section on team composition, the evidence for team-based selling is also mounting. Vendor operations that separate sales people from support service personnel – who have traditionally been responsible for customer satisfaction – nearly always create a *'churn & burn'* culture where the sales people are only interested in getting the order and then moving quickly onto the next sale. Again, this model is no longer sustainable and we are now heading increasingly towards coordinated team-based selling, and away from the traditional autonomous *'lone wolves'*. Many of today's advanced vendors are now creating *centrally coordinated teams*, where a more holistic approach to the account (pre and post sale) can be facilitated. If we agree with the concept that sales people can no longer attain 'trusted advisor' status with their customers, then why rely on one person to try to convince the target customer of the value proposition? *Insight selling* (as outlined by Adamson et al) suggests that vendors effectively need a *hit-squad* that can develop a coordinated approach to demonstrating real value to the customers.

I firmly believe that collaborative sales teams, built on shared responsibilities and competencies, will eventually become the new normal, and this further strengthens the case for *Sales Transformation*. At the very least, this new way of thinking suggests that sales leaders should conduct a full review of their sales execution strategy if for no other reason than to simply challenge the status-quo. Personally, I can see no alternative future for vendor sales than one that involves a much greater degree of team-based selling, and this will no doubt force vendors to re-think their hiring practices. Overhauling and improving talent management practices will also become a natural by-product of *Sales Transformation*.

Strategic alliances

In my experience, strategic alliance partnerships have mostly been about positioning and grand standing, despite the fact that, in the early days of this once very popular business trend, organisations could derive almost instantaneous share price increases through the announcement of an important strategic alliance. These alliances are supposed to be very close business relationships between two companies for their mutual benefit, however, my experience has not been a positive one with most of these partnerships failing to produce much, if any, value for either party.

The IT industry is littered with strategic alliances that have failed to produce anything and there are many well documented reasons for these failures. That said, we have learned, from the "'vendor stack'" concept, that developing *alliance* partnerships with other key vendors now has new meaning. In the future, vendors will be forced to invest more time and resource in ensuring that they are, at the very least, 'aligned' with the

I ('*prime*') vendors that supply each of their customers. This will involve a more strategic and methodical approach to developing close partnerships and alliances with the primary goal being to bolster the position within an account by having a powerful friend.

Like it or not, those vendors that are classified as Tier 2 or Tier 3 (or higher) will most likely have to relinquish some on-going margins in return for a the support of an influential Tier 1 partner. The truth is that these types of partnerships will always be difficult due to an unbalanced independence whereby the Tier 1 vendor will always have a greater relative power position. The Tier 3 vendor is much more dependent on the Tier 1 vendor and this presents its own set of challenges for sales leaders.

Sales Transformation - Next Steps:

1. Review and analyze the sales team composition and capabilities. Develop a skills matrix to clearly identify gaps in capability.

2. Frame the perfect sale – create a hypothetical sales opportunity for each product offering that brings together the optimal skill sets from across the current sales team at the critical points in the sales cycle. Use this hypothetical model to inform the *division of labor* and possible team-based selling scenarios.

3. Review sales force compensation against a team-based approach to selling, and begin to set expectations with sales team in this regard.

4. Create a dedicated strategic alliances function allowing sales people to capture '*vendor stack*' data for each account. Engage each Tier 1 ('*prime*') vendor for strategic alliance purposes, and be prepared to relinquish margin to these new-found friends.

Sales-Marketing Alignment:

Throughout my career, I have been constantly astonished at the disparity that often exists between the sales and marketing departments. This disparity or lack of alignment nearly always undermines sales execution along with company culture and the ripple effect often creates serious problems that can spill over to create negative customer perceptions. I have witnessed situations where the marketing and sales departments only speak to one another when they have to, and when they do, it is anything but pleasant. The connection between sales and marketing really should be a very natural collaboration but, for some reason, we often find a 'Chinese wall' between the sales and marketing departments, which absolutely impacts business performance. Why is this all too common barrier between sales and marketing allowed to develop? Why do the respective business leaders in both departments allow this counterproductive lack of alignment to exist?

Peter Strohkorb is a specialist international business consultant who has just published a book on this very topic of sales and marketing collaboration. Peter has developed something that he calls the *OneTeam Method*™ which argues that there has never been a time when sales and marketing personnel have needed to collaborate more closely, or effectively, than they do today, and I couldn't agree with him more.

Everyone accepts that sales and marketing executives are often driven and measured in different ways, and that these employees are often quite different types of people. However, to allow hostility to develop between these two highly-related and critically important business functions is simply an indictment on both the sales and marketing leaders, and senior management in general. You don't need to have read the latest thinking around management practices to realize that, when this type of division is left to fester between these two groups of people, it will eventually lead to a toxic culture where staff turnover and HR issues will become the norm. Again, flippantly, if your aim is to improve the businesses of your key competitors then by all means continue to allow this sales-marketing divide to exist. Put simply, sales and marketing must now collaborate more effectively and more often, and as Peter Strohkorb eloquently states: *"The degree to which your organisation collaborates, or does not collaborate, is the leading indicator of how well – or how poorly – your organisation is equipped to cope with the new buying paradigm"*.

When sales leaders fail to grasp the importance of the sales-marketing alignment they will face a very difficult future competing with vendors that get this right, and there is now clear evidence that demonstrates financial performance improvements can be delivered when sales and marketing are combined as one team.

New tools

Best practice sales organisations in 2015 are now aligning their business around the customer by harnessing the collective knowledge, data and insights of the team and associated third parties to improve sales productivity. With digital channels, we have shifted from traditional sales and marketing vehicles to a more social and viral approach. The use of *Big Data*, predictive analytics, social media, blogs and various forms of social *'listening'* are fast becoming standard tools in the armory of vendors for not just creating 'awareness' and more targeted selling, but also for ensuring that vendors know exactly what customers (and competitors) are saying about them. One of the most powerful ways of using social media is to get customers to recommend products to one another, and this will help build awareness and ensure vendor 'mind-share' throughout the *buying journey*. Building strong customer relationships, turning customers into advocates and working with a sense of urgency and pace to manage bad experiences will all build trust and help avert disaster when times are tough.

IT buyers of the future will progressively turn to social media and the likes of *YouTube* for information rather than calling a vendor sales person, and these tools will become more important for vendor sales teams to master as they try to provide a high quality customer experience. *Saleforce.com*'s own sales personnel utilize some custom-built *'chatter'* tools to provide their sales people with a more complete picture of their customers, and this is exactly the sort of innovation that can uncover those veritable *gold nuggets* of information which can sway a deal in a sales person's favor. In order for sales people to be successful in this customer-led era, they will have to rely more heavily on leveraging the network of contacts connected to the vendor business. As previously outlined, *cold calling* is now only useful if your aim is to annoy people, thus sales people must establish a different approach to finding a connection with the target customer.

As everyone knows, social media tools help facilitate networking on a greater scale than previously imagined, and any sales person operating in the new customer-led era that is not leveraging these tools is being outgunned by those that do. In my experience, *LinkedIn* is one of the most underutilized services that is currently available to sales and marketing people, although I believe that this is slowly changing as more vendors become aware of the declining results from blanket marketing and *cold calling*. The really savvy salespeople are increasingly using *LinkedIn* as a primary source of new leads and tangible revenue-generating opportunities. In fact, when it comes to B2B sales, *LinkedIn* is a critical tool that can make sales prospecting faster, smoother and more profitable. Beyond simply searching for sales connections (and yes, connections breed connections), some of the underutilized features of *LinkedIn* are Polls, Display Ads, Recommendation Ads, Targeted Status Updates, and Partner Messages.

Of course, relying on tools (as powerful as some can be), will never replace the people and process elements of effective sales execution. Technology won't be enough without a cohesive team of sales people, and more importantly, a cohesive team that understands the current implications of the new *buying journey*.

'Big Data'

Ongoing advancements in data management and computing power has helped create new tools for sales leaders to glean insights that can increase sales effectiveness. However, converting *Big Data* into useful and actionable data, is still an obstacle faced by many businesses, creating a gap between data availability and data usefulness.

Because sales people spend a large percentage of their time searching for customer-related information, usually prior to making their calls, it is now important to implement a process for collecting data relevant to your industry and customers. To that end, there now exists a wide range of data analytics services that can greatly assist sales people in filtering through all the noise: IBM's Watson Analytics, Google Analytics, InsightSquared, Canopy Labs, Tranzlogic, and Qualtrics to name just a few. Big data is a way for sales leaders to move beyond traditional CRM tools and can help with micro-segmentation, sentiment analysis, customized cross/up selling and even location based selling.

Put simply, effective use of Big Data can provide sales people with data insights that include being able to 1) identify customers that have the most value or potential value, 2) identify cross/up-selling opportunities, and 3) determine optimal sales approaches. In my experience as a sales leader, the one thing that we are always trying to achieve is a sales productivity improvement and this usually translates to more time spent selling, and less time spent crunching data and researching. In that sales context, the benefits of Big Data seem obvious, however, there are often many organizational and intellectual obstacles. Solutions to these obstacles will become clearer through increased commitment to specific initiatives that will help cultivate collaboration and data sharing internally – collecting meaningful data, rigorous analyses, developing trained teams to adhere to collection and analysis processes, and team-wide buy-in to invest in data-driven processes. The key to Big Data, as it pertains to B2B sales, is to keep the end goal in mind. That is, how do you gather appropriate, meaningful and relevant data that can become useful information for sales execution?

Sales Transformation– Next Steps:

1. Realign sales and marketing objectives to ensure enhanced collaboration between these two critical business functions.

2. Investigate the use of new data analytics services and tools (social media and *'Big Data'*) that can assist sales productivity, whilst also guarding against competitive threats.

3. Establish a *'Big Data'* task force to examine data sources and processes that can aggregate valuable sales information. Begin with the end in mind.

4. Engage a LinkedIn professional to train sales staff on the effective use of all LinkedIn functionality.

5. Convert customers into advocates – invest additional resource in ensuring high levels of customer satisfaction. Provide a handful of key customers with some free value-add in return for their advocacy.

Sales Force Compensation (SFC):

Not a lot has changed when it comes to the way that sales people are compensated. During my career, spanning almost three decades, each and every compensation plan that I have followed has been based on a *percentage of sales revenue* calculations. Having now spent 15+ years managing sales teams, I'm increasingly frustrated by how much time the average sales manager must spend listening to sales people complain about their 'comp plan'. Worse still, I'm now convinced that this problem is about to get even worse for many vendors due to the increased tightening of all sales-related costs that follow as a natural consequence of maturing markets and increasing competition. Don't get me wrong, the design, development and execution of an effective 'comp plan' is not only difficult, but it really should continuously evolve in parallel with business and market changes.

In the past, successful IT sales people could quite literally earn a fortune, sometimes simply for being in the right place at the right time. However, as the industry matures, competition intensifies and this creates downward pressure on margins making it very difficult for IT sales people to earn the sorts of commissions that they earned in the past. Increased financial pressure now means that many IT vendors are scrambling to identify areas where the cost of sales can be reduced, and SFC has always been a critical piece of the sales execution strategy – not to mention the fact that it is a large cost that must be managed effectively.

Given the increased attention now being paid to SFC, it is not surprising that it is now also gaining more and more attention from the world of academia with some enlightening empirical research beginning to be made available. Professor Doug J. Chung has spent many years studying the theory and practice of how companies can and should manage and pay salespeople – research that he now continues at Harvard Business School. Chung now has clear evidence that:

- Setting and adjusting quotas is nearly always done without sufficient analysis. It is important to keep quotas at the right level to properly motivate sales people.

- Arbitrary caps imposed on overachievement are detrimental. Companies sell more when they eliminate thresholds, gateways and milestones.

- "Ratcheting" quotas up following attainment in the previous period severely impacts motivation.

In my personal experience, these important points (above) resonate loudly. Simplicity is always preferable – the more complex the 'comp plan' the more difficult and costly it is to manage and administer, and this complexity almost always seems to impact the motivation of sales people. Sales staff attrition has always been a massive problem with vendor organisations (one that is deserving of more serious attention), and this problem is about to become an even bigger problem within the context of the customer-led era where high competition and decreasing profits are commonplace. These are some of the reasons that I believe that SFC is now a critical component to effective sales execution and one of the most important elements in a successful staff retention strategy. Some vendors are now basing a portion of the SFC on various customer satisfaction metrics – such as Net Promoter Scores (NPS), etc. – and I have no doubt that rewarding these types of behaviours will become increasingly prevalent moving forward.

Consumption Economics (Wood *et al*, 2011) is a book that clearly portrays a transition from large upfront sales transactions, where sales people are paid large one-off commissions 30 days after the customers purchase order is received, to a new model where smaller, more recurring "micro-transactions" will become the norm. As a result of the transition to some of these new models, SFC must be reviewed. Natural market forces are the *invisible hand* of every market and some vendor CEOs are now arguing that SFC should be reduced to match the changed market conditions and the somewhat diminished role of the sales person in this context. Not only is this perfectly understandable, but it's yet another reason that vendors should conduct a wholesale review of SFC.

The challenge here for vendors will be in reengineering 'comp plans' to ensure that motivation is not lost, and that key sales staff are retained during what might become a period of prodigious turbulence for many vendors. Personally, I cannot see how it will be possible for vendors to begin the process of *Sales Transformation* without including SFC as a key agenda item.

To break it down, rewards must be aligned with the desired behaviours and, given that the desired behaviours of vendor sales people is changing rapidly, SFC must now be revised to ensure that it is relevant and appropriate (and implementable), in the changing circumstances. A well-designed SFC plan is supposed to encourage certain desired behaviours and this reminds me of a very well-known business author, Mr Steven Kerr (1995), and his now famous article *"On the Folly of Rewarding A while Hoping for B"*. It was one of those rare cases where the title succinctly captures a concept to which most business leaders can instantly relate. Kerr's central point is that we can only expect people to rationally do (or pretend to do) the things that are rewarded rather than the things we say they should do. As the old saying goes: *"Always put your money on self-interest...at least you know the jockey is trying"*.

Sales Transformation - Next Steps

1. Pending other decisions made on transforming business models, review SFC to ensure rewards are aligned with desired behaviours.

2. Amend SFC to include incentives for team-based or collaborative selling.

3. Establish a new approach to compensation that rewards on-going customer contact to ensure continuity of relationship and high levels of customer satisfaction.

4. Eliminate any existing thresholds, gateways and milestones in SFC. Simplicity is the key.

www.transformsales.com.au

Coaching for Change

Confucius once said (apparently): *I hear and I forget, I see and I remember. I do and I understand.* This resonates loudly with me when it comes to the art of selling. Supporting this *Confucian* concept is the fact that many studies now show that adults retain about 65 percent of experiential learning compared with just 10 percent of material they receive in a lecture setting or in demonstrations. Throughout my career I have been exposed to, and trained in, almost every sales technique and methodology that has been developed, and all of this training has amounted to nothing when compared with the lessons learned from actually going out into the field and selling. I have made practically every mistake there is to make when it comes to selling, and there is no doubt that I have learned more from these mistakes than from any of the high priced sales training programs that I have undertaken. Short form training programs are better than doing nothing but, if the learnings are not continually practised, then they are gradually forgotten.

I'm now also certain that I could have learned many of the important sales lessons much faster if I had been given access to an experienced coach or mentor. Most of my early career was spent behaving as an autonomous agent *(lone wolf)* out in the field hunting alone within a defined patch. Many of the sales managers that I have worked for have simply been a sales peer that was promoted on the back of a couple of good years, and we all know that a great player doesn't always make a great coach. Moreover, almost all of my managers have been reactive and obsessed with short term results that they rarely made time (or, more likely, had the skills) to become an effective coach or mentor. At its core, good coaching is about much more than going on a *ride-along* with your team or doing a sales pitch while someone watches. It's about a genuine long term commitment to improving your people by providing constructive feedback, empathizing, helping them work through issues, and reinforcing their strengths. Effective coaching is also about creating the right culture for personal development, modeling new behaviours and helping to inspire a shared vision.

Managers and leaders in the organization can be as effective as externally hired coaches. However, successfully adapting to changed circumstances comes from breaking old habits, and turning sales managers into effective coaches often requires some important changes in behaviour. Some companies have found that a structured coaching program with at least weekly contact between coach and salesperson is vital to changing how people work. One of the vendors that I interviewed recently provided their sales managers with training in traditional skills such as handling difficult conversations and they assigned a "super-coach" for each sales person, and the company credits this enhanced coaching role with a 15 percent improvement in conversion rates.

Obviously, specialist human resources are costly, and I'm not suggesting that a coach must be sourced externally. However, unless organisations are willing to invest in on-going coaching and or mentorship programs, then their sales people are destined to make all of the same costly mistakes that I made throughout my career.

Sales Transformation programs (small or large) that involve substantive behavioural change will have a greatly improved chance of succeeding when the sales teams can acquire regular and frequent contact with a professional coach. It is therefore my view that coaching and mentoring of sales personnel will become even more critical for success in the future where competition thrives and where disruptive change is a constant.

Sales Transformation - Next Steps:

1. Identify a suitable sales professional who can perform the role as coach/mentor to sales people.

2. Ensure that the coach is closely aligned with the business objectives.

3. Create an on-going coaching program to ensure sustainable behavioural change.

www.transformsales.com.au

CHAPTER 12

Conclusion and Re-cap:

It's now clear that the big challenge for vendors is how to bridge the chasm that now exists between the new buying journey and the old B2B sales models. Since John H Patterson first developed the B2B sales models in 1884, the sales function has always been an important part of the value creation process for most businesses. The classic view of a *value ladder* has nearly always depicted sales as one of many business functions that helped to increase perceived customer value through the process of assisting customers to solve complex problems, and thus converting prospective customers into top-line revenue. This book now clearly points to a new world order where sales is no longer seen (in many cases) as adding, but instead, eroding value by failing to keep pace with the way in which customers now wish to buy complex technology products.

Value ladder diagrams - Sales is now eroding value for vendor organisations.

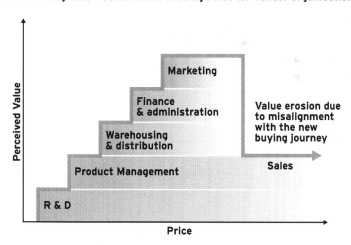

Broadly speaking, we are witnessing an accelerated divergence of customer and vendor interests, which means that vendor sales departments are now too often focused on the wrong activities and objectives. Short term thinking continues to drive a wedge between sales teams and the customers that they are meant to be serving. The way customers perceive value is changing and sales people will have to rise to the challenge of selling a full-lifetime service in a circular economy rather than just selling a product and moving on. Sophisticated and well-educated customers are no longer interested in the traditional sales models as markets continue to evolve and mature across the majority of the IT industry.

For almost three decades, I have attempted to continuously improve my knowledge and skills as a sales person and, during that time, one thing has remained universally true: Customer tastes and preferences (that is, buyer behaviour) is what drives markets. As has been asserted throughout this book, the traditional sales models that I have spent my career learning and executing are no longer relevant. Why? Because sales success is inexorably linked with the *buying journey* and the *buying journey* has changed from what I would describe as *vendor-push* to a *customer-pull* model. Customers are now in control and this means that vendors are now being called into **most** sales opportunities after 60%–80% of the customer decision-making process has already been completed. This radically changes the role of the vendor sales person, and this is the most serious change now impacting every vendor sales person – globally. If sales people can no longer influence buyer decision-making then what role do professional sales people now play?

The now common edict of doing *"more business with less vendors"*, coupled with the modern approach to the *'vendor stack"* are also major game changers for vendor sales people. As vendor rationalization continues to gain speed, most vendors are going to have to get used to the idea of aligning themselves with other Tier 1 vendor partners as a channel to their end-user and, as part of a protectionist strategy, that will hopefully improve customer retention. Put simply, any vendor that is currently categorized by a customer as a Tier 3 vendor (or higher) is now facing significant threats to their existing business models:

- Customers are now seeking to *cull* any Tier 3 vendors that may be seen as *'non-essential'*.
- Customers will increasingly request their Tier 3 vendors to engage only via a Tier 1 (*'prime'*) vendor in the future.

Either of the above scenarios means that the role of Tier 3 vendors (and that is the vast majority of vendors) is now under threat unless the vendor can find ways to climb up the *'vendor stack'* or increase its relevance and become more deeply embedded within the customer's technology ecosystem. Both of these scenarios require a vendor rethink, and the task for vendor sales people just keeps getting more and more difficult.

In addition to spending more time trying to add value with each of their accounts across the extended *buying journey*, vendor sales people must now also begin to collaborate with the Tier 1 (*'prime'*) vendors within each account. Developing these external partner relationships may not produce any additional short term revenue returns (in fact some will result in decreased revenues through margin erosion), but these alliances will help protect against the increasing likelihood of being *culled* from a key account.

Technology buyers are rapidly adopting *consumption-based* models and *XaaS* and this will also mean that vendors that are not already doing so will soon be forced to develop, and actually implement, programs that support *risk sharing* and more *flexible* pricing and delivery models. This will undoubtedly mean that vendors will be less profitable in the short term and this remains the biggest challenge for vendor CEOs as they continue to grapple with equity-owning shareholder expectations and the stock market indicators that value their businesses and, of course, impact their own compensation plans.

Depending on which analyst you subscribe to, the jury remains out on the real profitability that can be derived from these *consumption based* models. However, one thing is certain, vendors that fail to embrace these new pricing and delivery models will be gradually marginalized and replaced by vendors that are prepared to put some *'skin in the game'* by offering risk share/revenue share and genuine flexibility to their customers.

Top 10 Next Steps

1. Vendors must become 'market sensing' – paying greater attention to rapidly evolving customer requirements.

2. Vendor sales people must stop tracking the sales cycle and start tracking the new buying journey. Vendor sales people must identify when they are entering the buying journey late – being used as 'column fodder' destroys conversion rates and therefore company value.

3. Vendors must clarify exactly where they rank on each customers 'vendor stack'. Failure to understand the 'vendor stack' and unique vendor procurement policies creates significant risk for vendors.

4. Vendors must pay greater attention to qualifying sales opportunities, and be prepared to rapidly *qualify out*. Revolutionizing the approach to creating awareness is now critical – cold calling is dead, and solution selling is on the way out.

5. Vendor businesses will benefit by involving sales people in the key financial metrics that are used to measure and manage their businesses. AOV and ASCT are examples of two simple levers that can result in rapid uplift in sales performance.

6. Vendors must identify ways to refocus away from short-term revenue results and place greater emphasis on more equitable and sustaining customer relationships. Business models must be modified to create increased flexibility for customers.

7. Vendor sales leaders must leverage all of the unique skills and knowledge within their teams. Team-based selling and collaboration will soon become the new normal for structuring and organizing a distributed sales force.

8. Vendor sales departments must align more closely with internal marketing whilst leveraging new tools like social media and

Big Data analytics. Focus on new ways of converting customers into advocates.

9. Vendor compensation plans must be revised to provide incentives that are congruent with transformed structures and organizational objectives. Simplicity is the key.

10. Sales personnel will require a greater degree of coaching and mentoring as the role of the B2B sales person rapidly evolves – 130 years of the same approach to B2B sales has created behaviours and habits that must be undone. Professional coaches will be critical to sales success in the new customer age.

It will always be difficult to convince those vendors that are still growing and profitable based on the old sales models that there is now an urgent need for change. And I'm happy to acknowledge that some elements of my Top 10 Initiatives are much easier said than done. However, there are a number of very simple *quick wins* that will be easily applied for almost every IT vendor business. Creating an *"outside-in perspective"* which places actual customer requirements and market trends at the heart of the business is not difficult to implement. Developing a focus on financial metrics (like AOV and ASCT) and a new approach to *qualifying* can also be implemented immediately with little or no impact on short term revenue results. Working more closely with marketing personnel to build better awareness programs and to leverage new tools like social media and *Big Data* are also not difficult. Rethinking sales force compensation and engaging a coach are not insurmountable tasks. The most difficult aspect of Sales Transformation, as I see it, will be enacting any sweeping changes to vendor business models that impact short term financial performance expectations. Asking any business person or shareholder to accept greatly reduced returns on investment in the short term in the hope that returns will be higher in the long term is never going to be an easy task. However, I'm reminded of what Nelson Mandela once said: *"It always seems impossible until it's done".*

Where to start? Well, the reality is that not all vendors will embrace all of the suggestions outlined in this book. However, at the very least, I'm hopeful that I have provided some *food for thought* and some concepts that can be cherry-picked by vendor sales leaders depending on their current levels of business maturity. For some vendors, creating an uplift in sales productivity will be as simple as taking a more rigorous approach to *qualifying*. For others, a more holistic approach to *Sales Transformation* will be required. Regardless of which of my Top 10 Initiatives are embraced there is one thing of which I'm certain: Changing nothing and expecting a different result is madness.

Like any transformative change (small or large) this kind of organizational rethinking and restructuring will, in some cases, require a very carefully planned and executed approach to a sustaining change management program. *Sales Transformation* is absolutely not a series of revolutionary (big bang) changes, nor should it be highly disruptive. To be successful, this type of business transformation will require a methodical, incremental and sustainable approach to change. Will there be resistance? Of course, and, whilst I'm happy to concede that it's logical to keep doing what once made your company successful, let me be clear, *Sales Transformation* is not an optional 'nice-to-have' – it's a 'catch-up' play, and having senior execs involved is a critical success factor in driving this type of sustainable change.

Doing nothing – that is, making no changes to your current sales execution strategy – is a sure fire path to obscurity. My hope is that the key takeaways are clear: Upheaval and change now characterize the current global outlook for vendors and rapidly adapting to these changes will be crucial to survival. One final time – for businesses that continue to rely on a B2B sales model that was devised 130 years ago, it is now time to wake up and get with the program. Vendors must now be willing and able to break with tradition and make some important changes that begin to address the *new buying journey*. Vendors must become more agile, lean, adaptive and customer-centric if they are to survive and thrive into the future. As Charles Darwin said, it's not the strongest that survive, it's the most adaptable to change, and those vendors that remain stuck in the centuries old B2B sales models, satisfied with the *status-quo,* are now facing a very grim future unless they begin the process of rapid *Sales Transformation.*

C. Michael Armstrong – former CEO of AT&T – was referring to the increasingly globalized economy when he famously stated: *"In the future there will be two kinds of organisations; those that go global and those that go bankrupt".* Along those lines, it is my contention that the key findings and associated implications outlined in this book also create two diametrically opposed groups of IT vendor organisations: Those that embrace the abovementioned changes and transform, and those that go out of business.

"The soft-minded man always fears change. He feels security in the status quo, and he has an almost morbid fear of the new. For him, the greatest pain is the pain of a new idea."

– Martin Luther King Jr.

References

1. 451 Research – *2014 M&A Outlook* (by Brenon Daly) – view on the 24th of Feb, 2014. [www.451research.com/report-short?entityId=79949&referrer=marketing]

2. Adamson, Dixon and Toman – *The End of Solution Sales* – Harvard Business Review (July-August, 2012).

3. Accenture –Connecting the Dots on Sales Performance Report – published May 2012. [www.accenture.com/accenture-connecting-dots-sales-performance.pdf]

4. ACG Research – *Managed Service Cloud Opportunity Report 2009 (By Lauren Robinette) – viewed on the 2nd or March, 2014.*

5. CIO Website – *Where is IT Outsourcing headed in 2013?* (By Rebecca Merrett), published 16th of October, 2012 – viewed on 2nd of March 2014.

6. Department of Foreign Affairs and Trade (DFAT) – *The Importance of Services Trade to Australia*, viewed on 2nd of March, 2014[www.dfat.gov.au]

7. Frost & Sullivan Research (as cited by ITWire) – *Cloud services adoption on the up in Australia*(by Peter Dinham), viewed on 10th of October, 2013. [www.itwire.com/it-industry-news/strategy/61473-cloud-services-adoption-on-the-up-in-australia>

8. Gartner – *Demand for Cloud-Based Offerings Impacts Security Service Spending Report* (by Eric Alhm – published 3rd of April 2013), viewed on 28th of December, 2013 [www.gartner.com/doc/2408215/demand-cloudbased-offerings-impacts-security]

9. Gartner– *Key Challenges in IT Cost Optimization* – view on the 24th of February, 2014, [www.gartner.com/technology/topics/it-cost-optimization.jsp]

10. Investopedia.com – *industry lifecycle definitions* – view on the 12th of December, 2013. [www.investopedia.com/terms/i/industrylifecycle]

11. International Data Corporation (IDC) – *Australia Cloud Services 2013–2017 Analysis and Forecast* (by Raj Mudaliar – published July 2013), viewed on the 22nd of January 2014, [www.idc.com/getdoc.jsp?containerId=AU2577409V]

12. IDC – *Australian ICT Growth Driven by 3rd Platform Technologies Report (#AU245803)*, 6th of February, 2014, viewed on 23rd of February 2014. [www.idc.com]

13. KPMG International – *KPMG's Global Automotive Executive Survey 2014* – [www.kpmg.com/global/en/issuesandinsights/articlespublications]

14. PricewaterhouseCoopers International Ltd – *Analysis and trends in US technology M&A activity 2013 Report* (published February 2013), viewed on the 24th of January 2014 [www.pwc.com/us/en/transaction-services/publications/us-technology-mergers-acquisitions].

15. Prelytix.com – *The new reality of the B2B sales process* – infographic. Viewed on 22nd of February, 2015 [www.prelytix.com/reality-b2b-sales-process-infographic]

16. Technology First Magazine – *What is the 3rd Platform, and how will it affect business?* (By Mark Neistat), viewed on the 25th of February, 2104 <www.technologyfirst.org/magazine-articles/124-may-2013/843-mark-neistat-us-signal-company>

17. TechTarget Report, April 2010 – Search CIO website – viewed on the 6th of February, 2014. [www.searchcio.techtarget.com]

18. The Economist Intelligence Unit Ltd 2013 – *The rise of the customer-led economy Report* (published: December 3rd 2013), viewed on the 3rd of March, 2014 [www.economistinsights.com/analysis/rise-customer-led-economy]

19. Wood.J.B et al – *B4B: How Technology and Big Data Are Reinventing the Customer-Supplier Relationships,* published by Point B, Inc. (November 1, 2013).

20. Wood.J.B et al – *Consumption Economics: The New Rules of Tech,* published by Point B, Inc. (November 1, 2011).

21. Roff-Marsh, J – *The Machine, A radical approach to the design of the sales function* – published by Ballistix, 2011

22. Strohkorb, P – *The One Team Method* – published by Peter Strohkorb (2015)

23. Yip, George S. & Bink, Audrey J.M.– *Managing Global Customers – An Integrated Approach,* published by Oxford University Press (2007).

About the Author:

With more than 27 years in B2B sales and sales leadership roles, Graham Hawkins is a highly-experienced and versatile business executive with proven strengths in strategic business development, go-to-market planning and sales & marketing in general. Graham has worked in the UK, Australia and across Asia Pacific as a representative of some of the most innovative organisations in IT, Telecommunications, Finance and Media. Graham has extensive experience in developing, mentoring and leading highly-successful sales teams whilst embracing and driving multi-channel sales engagement strategies.

Today, Graham is the Founder and CEO of *Transform Sales International* (**www.transformsales.com.au**), a specialist consulting firm that assists small, medium and large organisations with strategic sales planning, business development and sales force optimization.

Graham has an MBA (*Distinction*) from RMIT and is a member of *Golden Key* – International Honor Society for high performing business students. Through his company, *Transform Sales International*, Graham now works with CEOs, Sales & Marketing executives and Entrepreneurs, to assist in driving *Sales Transformation* programs and best practices that help ensure business performance and sustainability.

Graham Hawkins

Sales and Business Development Professional

Email: graham@transformsales.com.au

Website: www.transformsales.com.au

Acknowledgements:

Prue Jacobson: *former Head of Technology Procurement and Supplier Management* – **Qantas.**

Craig Brown: *former Commercial Vendor Manager – Procurement* – **National Australian Bank.**

Diane Fernley-Jones: *former CIO of* **Leighton Holdings Limited**

Paul Cameron: *former Executive General Manager of IT–* **Suncorp Limited.**

Dal McNamara: *Head of Procurement & Vendor Management* – **Westpac Banking Corporation.**

Greg Hunt: *Senior Manager – IT Asset and Inventory Management* – **Telstra.**

David Parry-Jones: *VP & GM UK & Ireland* – **VMware.**

Kevin Van Gils: *Director, Partners & Alliances* – **CA Technologies.**

Wendy Hamson: *former Director of Sales* – **SUSE.**

Simon Horrocks: *VP, Asia Pacific & Japan* – **ScienceLogic.**

Kim Jenkins: *former Managing Director, Australia & New Zealand* – **Experian Group.**

John Merakovsky – *Managing Director, Australia & New Zealand* – **Experian Group**

Hamish Miles: *former Director of Sales – Australia* – **Novell Corporation.**

Alan (Kingy) King: *Founder and CEO* – **A2Zoutcomes**.

Andrew Humphries: *Dealmaker – Global Entrepreneur Programme* – **UK Trade & Investment.**

Special thanks go to:

Prue Jacobson for inadvertently providing me with the inspiration to write this book. Your candour and insight set the wheels in motion for this book.

Rachael Hawkins, (my wife) for her extraordinary work as a wife and mother which has created the opportunity and time to allow me to write this book. I will always be grateful for your love and support.

Deidre Hawkins (my mother) for her encouragement and advice into the process of writing and producing a book. Mum, you continue to be my inspiration.

Note: The views expressed herein are solely those of the author and not of the organisations mentioned throughout this book.

Made in the USA
Middletown, DE
30 October 2016